Webfl

Wizardry

Design Stunning Websites and Landing Pages the No-Code Way

By Daniel Melehi

©2025

Contents

4

Webflow Wizardry: Design Stunning Websites and Landing Pages the No-Code Way

INTRODUCTION

I still remember the very first time I stumbled upon Webflow. I was on a hunt for a tool that would let me craft beautiful, professional-looking websites without painstakingly writing lines of code late into the night. That search led me to numerous platforms and possibilities, each one promising me the moon. But it was Webflow that pulled me in like a magnet. The intuitive layout, the subtle aesthetics, and of course, the promise of building pixel-perfect websites with minimal code—it all felt like I had struck gold.

At first, I was skeptical. How could a no-code tool really deliver the power and flexibility I craved? I had tried website builders before. They often came with major limitations or forced me into cookie-cutter templates that stifled my creativity. But with Webflow, things felt different. The interface welcomed me like a blank canvas, eager for fresh ideas. Drag-and-drop elements were only the beginning. The platform allowed me to toggle between a visual interface and deeper settings, letting me refine my designs to a professional standard.

That initial excitement quickly blossomed into a full-blown journey of discovery. I created my first landing page for a fashion startup, experimenting with subtle hover animations and bold typography that demanded attention. The entire process felt both intuitive and thrilling. I didn't need to spend hours wrestling with custom CSS to achieve a modern layout. Instead, Webflow gave me a robust set of tools, from adjustable breakpoints for responsive design to powerful interactions that breathed life into my pages.

It was at that moment I realized: no-code design isn't just about making things easier—it's about freeing creative energy to focus on the user experience and brand storytelling. Instead of being bogged down with technicalities, I could pour my heart and soul into the design process. Whether I was selecting the perfect color palette or prototyping dynamic scrolling effects, my mind buzzed with new possibilities. And that's precisely why I decided to write this book, "**Webflow Wizardry: Design Stunning Websites and Landing Pages the No-Code Way**."

In the upcoming chapters, I want to take you along on a rich, first-person narrative through everything you need to know about Webflow. We'll begin with the foundational mindsets and no-code design principles, then venture into the platform's dashboard and features. Together, we'll examine how to structure projects from the ground up, explore design best practices, and discover how to implement crucial components such as the box model. Each step of the way, I'll share relatable stories and hard-earned insights I've picked up along my own journey, offering you a roadmap to help you navigate the platform with confidence.

This book is designed for anyone who is passionate about visual storytelling but doesn't want to get tangled in the complexities of coding. If you're an entrepreneur, a designer, or even someone who simply loves creating engaging online spaces, you're in the right place. By the end of our time together, you'll be armed with the knowledge and skillset to produce truly immersive digital experiences—sites and landing pages that not only look incredible but also function flawlessly across a wide range of devices.

So, let's dive in. Let's embrace the no-code revolution hand in hand, unlocking new realms of creativity. In the pages to come, I'll guide you every step of the way, from the spark of an idea to a dazzling finished project that will leave clients, customers, and visitors wondering how you did it.

Let's get started on this exciting journey into the world of Webflow wizardry.

CHAPTER 1: EXPLORING NO-CODE DESIGN PRINCIPLES

When I first dipped my toes into the no-code realm, my mind was fixated on one burning question: "Is it truly possible to create high-caliber websites without writing code?" This skepticism quickly melted away as I discovered the core philosophies behind no-code design. The concept may sound magical at first, but to me, it's less about instant shortcuts and more about harnessing intuitive visual tools that empower creative minds.

What drove my fascination with no-code approaches was the prospect of focusing on user experience and storytelling rather than wrestling with syntax. Traditional coding processes can often derail our creativity, forcing us to juggle technical details instead of refining the overall vision. No-code design principles flip the script: imagine a painter who can seamlessly choose colors, brush strokes, and composition without having to assemble the canvas or mix chemical solutions first. In this way, we shift our mental bandwidth from "How do I build it?" to "What do I want to build?"

In the heart of these principles lies the drive for accessibility. Whether you're someone just starting out in web design or a seasoned developer looking for a more rapid workflow, no-code solutions bring web creation closer to everyone. Gone are the days when a single glitch in your stylesheet could derail an entire project. Instead, no-code emphasizes visual representation, letting you see your website spring to life in real time. This interactive feedback loop nurtures experimentation: you can test layouts, colors, and interactions on the fly, discarding or refining them instantly if they don't align with your vision.

No-code philosophies also champion experimentation and iteration. Early on, I learned the importance of prototyping. In a matter of minutes, I could sketch a header, drop in a hero image, add a call-to-action button, and see how the page responded on various devices—all without typing out a single line of code. This rapid prototyping frees you to explore multiple directions. If something doesn't work, you can revert without fuss. In contrast, code-heavy projects can tie you down to rigid structures that are time-consuming to undo.

But make no mistake—no-code doesn't equate to "no-control." Webflow, in particular, offers advanced styling options and the flexibility to insert custom code if you ever want to push the boundaries further. Still, the backbone of no-code remains user-centric design. These principles encourage you to think with empathy: "What does my visitor need?" "How can I streamline their experience?" When coding isn't monopolizing your time, you naturally channel your energy into refining user journeys, brand storytelling, and aesthetics that resonate.

One of my favorite aspects of no-code design is the sense of community. It's true that coding communities are vast and helpful, but the no-code space has a certain spark of camaraderie. Designers, entrepreneurs, and innovators share templates, tutorials, and creative hacks with genuine enthusiasm. This collective energy is infectious, fueling a culture where learning feels collaborative rather than competitive.

Overall, successful no-code design is about harnessing user-focused principles, embracing agile iterations, and blending creativity with functionality. In the chapters ahead, we'll apply these concepts within the framework of Webflow. From tinkering with the color scheme to ensuring the site is responsive, no-code fundamentals will provide the strong foundation you need to bring your ideas to life quickly—and have fun doing it.

Welcome to a new era of web creation, where everyone has a seat at the design table—no advanced coding knowledge required.

CHAPTER 2: NAVIGATING THE WEBFLOW DASHBOARD

I'll never forget the first moment I logged into the Webflow dashboard. It felt like stepping behind the scenes of a professional backstage area where stage lights, costumes, and accessories lined the walls—each one ready to be unleashed on the main stage. The dashboard is a hub teeming with design possibilities and organizational tools, all neatly sectioned so you can dive in without feeling overwhelmed.

When you first open Webflow, you land on the dashboard where all your projects live. It's essentially your control center, displaying thumbnails of your current sites, past experiments, and future ideas waiting in the wings. The layout is intentionally clean, featuring a top navigation bar that grants quick access to crucial resources like templates, design courses, and help guides. Over the years, I've found this intuitive arrangement to be an unsung hero. I can spot the project I need at a glance, clone or rename older versions, and even organize them into folders if the list starts to overflow.

On the left side, you'll notice tabs that handle your site's settings. These options guide you through domain setups, SEO settings, and backups. Think of it like the wings of a theater stage, where props and scenery wait to impress the crowd. The key is that everything is easy to find, letting you tweak your SEO titles before opening the designer or switch out domain configurations without a hitch.

One hidden gem I love is the ability to preview your project in different states. I can examine how a site appears in editing mode, toggle to the live version, or even investigate how it might look if I roll back to a previous backup. This multi-view approach is especially helpful when I experiment with changes but don't feel certain they'll enhance user experience. If something does go off the rails, I know I can revert in a flash.

Perhaps most thrilling is the direct path from the dashboard into the Designer, which is the visual interface where the bulk of the magic happens. Clicking into the Designer feels like stepping onto a stage with an array of creative tools at my disposal. But before we get into the details of shaping and styling elements, it's worth noting how each feature in the dashboard fits into the bigger picture. You have a clear line of sight from project inception to publication. You can set up hosting, tweak SEO basics, and manage backups all in one place. This end-to-end workflow is the hallmark of no-code efficiency.

Of course, the dashboard isn't just about managing. It's also a library of resources that can spark ideas. Webflow's template marketplace, directly accessible from the dashboard, gives you a peek at how professional designers tackle layouts, color schemes, and navigation structures. While I often prefer starting from a blank canvas, there's tremendous value in exploring templates to accelerate your workflow or to glean fresh inspiration. Even if you don't end up using a template, dissecting how it's built teaches you design patterns and best practices without a formal code lesson in sight.

Ultimately, getting comfortable with the Webflow dashboard is your ticket to a seamless, intuitive workflow. It's like the dressing room before a big performance, letting you gather all the items you need in one place, from domain settings to design assets. Once you feel at home in this space, you'll have the confidence to dive deeper into the next stages of building and designing.

Consider the dashboard your personal command center—reliable, organized, and ever-ready to support your creative ambitions.

CHAPTER 3: STRUCTURING YOUR FIRST PROJECT

The exhilaration I felt when I clicked "Create New Project" for the first time on Webflow can't be overstated. My mind buzzed with ideas: maybe I'd craft a slick portfolio page highlighting my design work, or set up a landing page for an upcoming product launch. Regardless of the end goal, the initial steps of structuring a project define how smoothly the creative process will unfold.

I like to think of structuring a Webflow project as building the scaffolding for a high-rise. If the scaffolding is solid, everything else can be layered on confidently. One of the first decisions you'll face is whether to start from a blank project or use a template. While templates offer a fantastic jump-start, sometimes it's empowering to start from scratch. By doing so, you'll gain a deeper understanding of the fundamental layers: sections, containers, and div blocks.

Sections are like major rooms in a house—each one can hold specific portions of your content, ensuring the design elements have a logical grouping. I usually begin by creating a top section for the site header, followed by another for the hero area, and continue downward for various content segments and a site footer. Containers step in like the walls that keep those rooms in order, offering structure for columns and text. Div blocks are even more flexible, enabling me to nest elements or apply custom styling.

Another key aspect of project structure is class naming—a strategy that helps maintain consistency throughout your design. Creating intuitive class names is more critical than many first-time Webflow users anticipate. Over time, I realized that using clear and descriptive names like "navbar-wrapper" or "featured-section" not only keeps my design files tidy but also helps me rapidly pinpoint elements later. This naming convention is especially valuable when you're juggling multiple pages or collaborating with others.

Speaking of collaboration, I've found that having a well-defined project structure can greatly reduce confusion if you're working with teammates. Shared naming strategies, consistent use of grid layouts, and labeling sections in a logical hierarchy make it a breeze for everyone to follow along. If a teammate jumps in to tweak a layout, they can identify the structure at a glance, avoiding messy or duplicated styles. This collaborative ease goes hand in hand with Webflow's no-code approach—design intelligence meets clarity, ensuring the project's creative heart doesn't get lost in chaos.

Now, let's talk about wireframing. While it's tempting to start adding fancy images and animations right away, there's real value in mapping out your site's layout before embellishing. I often create a quick wireframe using plain gray boxes to represent sections and placeholders for text. This way, I can test the flow and ensure the site's navigation makes sense. Once I'm happy with the skeletal layout, I replace those placeholders with real images, text, and styles. This step-by-step process ensures that the fundamental user journey remains the guiding light, rather than being overshadowed by design flourishes.

In essence, structuring a project effectively lays the foundation for everything else you'll build in Webflow. A well-organized framework saves time, fosters collaboration, and keeps the user experience front and center. Whether you're building a powerful e-commerce site or a simple personal blog, taking the time to plan sections, containers, and classes goes a long way in boosting your efficiency and ensuring a polished final product.

Every grand design needs a sturdy backbone. And in Webflow, that backbone is the structure of your project.

CHAPTER 4: UNDERSTANDING THE BOX MODEL IN WEBFLOW

Long before I ventured into Webflow, I heard designers and developers tossing around the term "box model." It sounded like a secret handshake in the coding world—something that, if you understood it, you'd unlock the mysteries of clean layout and consistent design. When I finally saw how Webflow implements the box model in a user-friendly interface, it felt like discovering a hidden superpower. Suddenly, a concept that once seemed reserved for seasoned coders was at my fingertips.

At its core, the box model is a way to think about how every element on a webpage occupies space. Each element—whether it's a paragraph, a button, or a container—can be viewed as a rectangular box. This box comprises the content area, plus optional padding, borders, and margins that define how it interacts with neighboring elements. In simpler terms, it's like layering boxes within boxes, each with its own set of spacing rules.

Padding is what I consider the cozy cushion around an element's content, ensuring text or images don't feel crowded against the edges. Borders, meanwhile, are the literal outlines around the box—useful for highlighting elements or creating clear separations. Margins are the gaps you leave between boxes. Once you visualize it this way, layering and alignment become more intuitive. I often use margin adjustments to space out sections on a webpage, ensuring the design "breathes" and doesn't appear cluttered.

In Webflow, you'll see a neat display of margin and padding controls in the right-hand style panel when you select an element. You can click and drag icons to increase or decrease spacing, or type in exact values if you're aiming for pixel-perfect precision. This live preview of spacing transforms the theory of the box model into a hands-on experience. If an element doesn't look quite right, I can adjust its margins or padding in real time and immediately see the impact.

One thing that took me some time to master was ensuring I didn't mix up margin and padding. Early on, I'd be adjusting the margin when I really needed to fine-tune the padding. To get comfortable, I'd sometimes layer color backgrounds or borders temporarily on elements so I could visually understand where each box began and ended. Once I recognized how the boxes nested within one another, I could apply consistent spacing without second-guessing myself.

Understanding the box model is crucial not only for making designs look neat but also for ensuring consistency across different screen sizes. Responsiveness often comes down to how well elements adapt to varying viewports. If you consistently use margin and padding settings, along with the appropriate display properties (such as Flex or Grid), you'll have fewer headaches down the line. When you move into smaller breakpoints, you can tweak these values to ensure your content remains readable and visually appealing on tablets and phones.

Mastering the box model is like learning to see the matrix of your webpage. Once you reframe your mindset to recognize each element as a box, the logic behind alignment and spacing becomes second nature. You'll know when to push elements apart using margins or when to nest them snugly via padding. This level of control is precisely why Webflow is a favorite among both novice and seasoned designers. You get the power of CSS layout concepts without having to memorize a sea of code.

So, don't let "box model" intimidate you. Embrace it, play with those boxes, and watch your designs snap effortlessly into the structure you envision.

CHAPTER 5: DESIGNING RESPONSIVE LAYOUTS

When I first recognized the significance of a responsive website, I was working on a personal portfolio that looked stunning on my laptop but clunky and disjointed on my phone. At that moment, I realized that modern web visitors expect a seamless experience across devices—laptops, tablets, and smartphones alike. In Webflow, the magic of responsive design awaits right beneath the surface, ready to transform a single layout into a versatile display that effortlessly adapts to multiple screen sizes.

My initial step toward responsive brilliance usually starts with the Desktop breakpoint. Here, I lay out my vision using containers, grids, and columns that structure my content. However, I keep a watchful eye on potentially tricky elements—like large hero images or wide pieces of text. It's easier to anticipate how these will scale if you plan ahead. Once I have a solid desktop design, I shift my focus to smaller viewports, clicking into Tablet and Mobile breakpoints within Webflow's Designer interface.

In my experience, designing for smaller screens is equal parts puzzle and art form. I pay attention to image sizes, which often need to shrink or stack neatly. Headlines frequently require smaller font sizes, and sometimes I tweak margins so that elements don't feel squished. One of my favorite Webflow features is the cascade of styles: changes I make at the desktop level trickle downward, but changes I make at a smaller breakpoint don't disrupt the larger ones. This layered approach means I don't have to rebuild each design from scratch at every viewport; instead, I refine and tailor as I go.

Beyond adjusting fonts and images, I also think strategically about the user experience (UX). For instance, on a mobile screen, a horizontal navigation bar might become a compact hamburger menu for better readability. Sliders that look gorgeous on a desktop can feel cumbersome on a phone if not properly optimized. To address these nuances, I often use Webflow's built-in interactions to hide or show elements based on screen size. It's not just beauty but also functionality that hinges on a responsive layout.

Another tip I picked up is to fine-tune the spacing—both horizontally and vertically—at different breakpoints. On smaller screens, less can be more. A single-column layout with enough breathing room often trumps a cluttered multi-column design. For me, whitespace isn't wasted space; it's an artful way to ensure the user can scan and digest information easily.

And then there's the matter of performance. High-resolution images perform beautifully on desktops with strong Wi-Fi, but they can bog down mobile devices. Whenever possible, I optimize my images or rely on Webflow's responsive image feature, which automatically generates scaled-down versions for various devices. This way, I maintain swift load times and keep visitors engaged, no matter the screen they're on.

Ultimately, crafting a responsive layout in Webflow is like choreographing a dance number with multiple sets of moves. Each step must be carefully tuned to fit the stage and the audience. With thoughtful planning and a willingness to adapt your design, you'll end up with a website that effortlessly dazzles on every device—and isn't that the goal of every modern website creator?

I've learned that a site's responsiveness can set it apart in a crowded digital space. It's not about compromising on design; it's about staying true to your core aesthetic while making sure every user can experience it in the best possible way.

CHAPTER 6: WORKING WITH ELEMENTS AND SYMBOLS

When it comes to building sites in Webflow, elements are the building blocks that bring my wildest designs to life. From headings and paragraphs to buttons and images, a well-placed element can capture attention and guide visitors through your narrative. But early on, I found myself reusing the same sets of elements over and over—adding headers, footers, or pricing layouts on multiple pages. That's precisely where Symbols stepped in, transforming repetitive tasks into moments of blissful design efficiency.

Before Symbols, I'd meticulously copy and paste elements from one page to the next. If I needed to tweak a detail, like updating a navigation link or adjusting a footer color, I had to hunt down each instance. The day I discovered Symbols in Webflow felt like a revelation. With one quick action, I turned my carefully crafted header section into a Symbol. Now, whenever I update that Symbol, the change cascades across every page where it appears. It's akin to flipping a single switch that lights up every room in your house.

Let's take a step back and look at the standard elements. Headlines (like H1 through H6) set the tone, giving me control over hierarchy and visual impact. Text blocks allow me to share more detailed information. Images and videos bring color and motion to the page, and buttons nudge my audience to take a desired action. Webflow organizes all of these elements in a handy sidebar. I treat it like a digital cabinet, stocked with everything I need to assemble a cohesive site.

But what if you're building something more complicated— like a card layout for featured products or a large hero section topped with a unique call to action? For tasks like these, custom div blocks become my best friend. A div block is essentially a blank container that can hold text, images, or other elements, and I can style it any way I want. I often pair div blocks with Flex or Grid layouts to achieve symmetrical, balanced designs or to create visually interesting asymmetrical patterns.

Once I've perfected a complex section, I can convert that entire structure into a Symbol. This might be a pricing table, a testimonial section, or anything else I plan to use across multiple pages. Symbols have saved me from countless repetitive edits, ensuring that my design remains consistent. If I decide to freshen up the color scheme or tweak a font size, I make the change once and trust that Webflow will handle the rest.

But Symbols aren't just about convenience; they're about nurturing a streamlined workflow. The less time I spend updating repeated sections, the more time I can devote to creative thinking—like fine-tuning micro-interactions or brainstorming new content ideas. Oftentimes, the difference between a good website and a great one lies in the little details that polish the user experience. Symbols free me to invest time in those details.

From day one in Webflow, I've come to see elements and Symbols as two sides of the same coin. Elements give me the power and precision to build, while Symbols amplify that power by letting me replicate and manage complex designs without lifting a finger. When these two functionalities are harnessed together, building a site transforms into a smooth, rewarding experience—one where I can focus on the magic of storytelling rather than the tedium of maintenance.

CHAPTER 7: MASTERING TYPOGRAPHY AND FONTS

I remember browsing typography sites late into the night, falling in love with the curves of a scripted font here or the modern crispness of a sans-serif typeface there. In my early design experiments, fonts were my secret weapon, dictating the personality of a site before a single image or color made its debut. In Webflow, mastering typography is as much an art as it is a science, and it starts with selecting the perfect font.

One of the first things I do in any new project is head straight to the Project Settings and connect Google Fonts or even custom font files I've sourced from platforms like Adobe Fonts. Why? Because typography sets the tone. A modern brand might need a sleek, geometric sans-serif, while a boutique bakery might thrive on a friendly, handwritten script. By defining these fonts upfront, I ensure each heading, paragraph, or button is brushed with the same consistent aesthetic.

Once I've chosen the right fonts, I refine their styling in the Designer. Webflow's interface allows me to adjust weight, line height, and letter spacing with near-instant feedback. I still remember the delight I felt the first time I used the real-time preview to find the perfect combination of boldness and spacing for a hero headline. Instead of guessing in code, I could see the effect unfold right before my eyes.

But it's not just about picking a fancy font and pushing it live. Readability matters. Large blocks of text quickly become draining to read if the line spacing is too tight or the color contrast is too low. My rule of thumb is to keep a comfortable line height—usually around 1.5 em or more—for paragraphs, especially if I'm dealing with long-form content like blog posts or case studies.

Hierarchy also plays a starring role in visual storytelling. I typically establish an H1 style for main titles, an H2 for section headings, and so on, each with its own font size and weight. This cohesive system ensures that even casual skimmers can glean key information at a glance. When everything from H2 to H6 follows a consistent pattern, the site flows naturally, guiding readers from one section to the next without confusion.

Let's talk about color, too. In Webflow, setting a global swatch for your text color can help maintain uniformity across all your headings and paragraphs. I might choose a rich charcoal hue for body text if I'm aiming for an elegant, polished look. For accent text—like calls to action—I sometimes choose a vibrant hue that ties beautifully into the overall brand palette.

One subtlety I've come to appreciate is the power of white space around text elements. Negative space not only makes the layout more inviting but also places emphasis on the wording itself. Sometimes, rather than crowding the page with graphics, I'll let the typography speak volumes. Even a simple combination of a tasteful serif heading and ample white space can convey sophistication.

All in all, typography is what gives a website its distinct character and tone. Thanks to Webflow's flexible styling panel, even those new to design can experiment with endless font combinations. To me, achieving typographical harmony in a project feels like hitting the perfect note: everything just resonates.

CHAPTER 8: CREATING ENGAGING VISUALS

The moment that truly hooked me on Webflow was when I saw how easily I could integrate compelling visuals into my layouts. Images, videos, and clever graphics have a magical ability to communicate mood, style, and narrative in a fraction of a second. But it's not just about throwing in eye candy; it's about weaving visuals into the fabric of the website so they tell a story as users explore.

My first stop for creating engaging visuals is often the hero section. This is where a full-width image or looping video can set the stage, greeting visitors with an immediate "wow" factor. Using Webflow's background video element is a breeze. By simply uploading a short looping clip, I can transform a static hero area into a dynamic, attention-grabbing section. That sense of motion not only looks polished but also communicates a mood—be it energizing, tranquil, or cutting-edge.

Of course, images are the staple of any website's visuals. Whether it's product shots for an e-commerce store or editorial images for a blog, quality counts. I typically prepare each photo by optimizing it for the web—balancing file size with clarity. Webflow's built-in responsive image feature helps by serving up the best possible resolution based on a visitor's device, so I don't have to worry about my crisp images becoming pixelated on smaller screens.

Sometimes, though, placing images alone isn't enough. I like to layer them with subtle overlays or pair them with text boxes that highlight crucial messages. In Webflow, it's easy to stack layers by adjusting positioning—Absolute, Relative, or Fixed—to achieve eye-catching compositions. Perhaps I feature a product shot in the background, then float a transparent box over it with a captivating headline. The result is a blended design that feels purposeful rather than random.

Let's not forget illustrations and icons. These smaller visual elements pack a punch when it comes to branding. An icon can instantly convey complex ideas—like shipping options or security—without forcing the user to sift through dense text. In my own workflow, I sometimes incorporate SVG icons for crisp scalability. Webflow's asset manager helps me stay organized, so it's straightforward to swap icons or refine color schemes as the design evolves.

One technique I've grown fond of is the use of image galleries or sliders for portfolio pages. With a slider, I can showcase multiple pieces of visual work while conserving valuable screen space. Webflow lets me customize transitions, whether I want a gentle fade or a dynamic slide, so the gallery feels like an integral part of the brand's personality.

As with any design element, moderation is key. Too many visuals can overwhelm users and slow down loading times. I try to strike a balance, focusing on a handful of strong, supportive images that complement the textual content. Sometimes minimalism works wonders, allowing each visual element to truly stand out.

In the end, visuals are the portal through which visitors experience the essence of your brand. With Webflow, creating engaging imagery becomes a joyful process, one where experimenting with size, layout, and animation is not only doable but genuinely fun. And for me, that's what keeps the spark of creativity alive each time I design a new project.

CHAPTER 9: USING INTERACTIONS AND ANIMATIONS

It was a simple hover effect that first caused me to realize the power of interactions in Webflow. I'd created a product card, and when visitors hovered over it, the card smoothly scaled up and revealed more details. That single movement—so subtle, yet so dynamic—transformed a static page into an engaging, story-driven interface. Moments like these taught me that animations and interactions aren't just decorative flourishes; they can guide users, highlight important information, and breathe life into a design.

Working with interactions in Webflow starts in the Interactions panel, where I can define triggers and actions. Triggers might be as simple as hovering over a button or as complex as scrolling through a long page. Each trigger can initiate a chain of effects—fading in elements, sliding them from off-screen, or changing background colors, to name just a few. This visual interface takes the mystery out of animation curves and timing. Rather than typing lines of code, I drag sliders or pick from dropdowns to shape my micro-interactions.

Take the navbar, for instance. I once built a sleek, disappearing navbar that only appeared once the user started scrolling back up. It was a small touch, but it kept the user's focus on the content while ensuring navigation remained easily accessible. In Webflow, designing this effect was simply a matter of selecting the navigation element, adding a "while scrolling" trigger, and setting keyframes that determined opacity and positioning.

Scrolling animations are another crowd-pleaser. Nothing captivates me more than a site that presents information piece by piece as I scroll down. I've created landing pages that gently introduce product features at timed intervals, letting the user digest content at a natural pace. By tying animations to scroll position, I can orchestrate a narrative journey, deciding which elements appear first and how they transition onto the screen.

One of my favorite tips: use interactions to focus attention. For example, a subtle pulsing effect on a "Sign Up" button can highlight a conversion goal, reminding users where to take action. Similarly, a floating call-to-action can catch the eye without being too aggressive. The trick is to keep animations smooth and purposeful. Too many flashing or bouncing elements can distract and even annoy your audience.

Performance also matters. While animations are dazzling, I ensure they don't negatively impact site speed. Generally, CSS-based animations and Webflow's built-in interactions are optimized to run smoothly across modern browsers, but I keep an eye on the complexity of each effect to avoid sluggish behavior on lower-end devices.

Finally, interactions are a chance to show off some personality. A playful brand might favor bouncy transitions, while a corporate site might embrace sleek, understated fades. Every movement reflects the website's tone and purpose. When I map out an interactions strategy, I imagine the site as a stage with its own choreography, each motion carefully designed to enhance the user's understanding and delight.

In short, using interactions and animations in Webflow can feel like adding a secret ingredient to a beloved recipe. It infuses each page with a sense of surprise and delight, ensuring users don't just scroll—they engage, immerse, and remember.

CHAPTER 10: BUILDING A ROBUST NAVIGATION MENU

Navigation menus have always felt like the backbone of any website I build. Long before I discovered Webflow, I would spend hours trying to piece together a menu that made sense, only to find it looked completely different on mobile devices. With Webflow in the picture, however, I finally found a more elegant approach. For me, crafting a robust navigation menu isn't just about the technical aspect; it's about guiding visitors with clear, intuitive paths.

My process usually starts with a clear vision of the site's hierarchy. I map out what pages need top-level placement— like Home, About, Services, and Contact—and which might sit under a dropdown, such as Resources or Blog. Webflow's Designer then makes it straightforward to transform this initial structure into a functional menu. I typically drag in a Nav Bar component as a starting point. This component feels like a ready-made skeleton that I can easily customize.

Next comes the styling. Webflow gives me granular control over everything, from the background color of the nav bar to the spacing of the menu links. If I'm going for a minimal look, I might set a semi-transparent background that lets a hero image peek through. If I need something bold, I'll consider a contrasting color to ensure the menu stands out on every page. It's remarkable how these small tweaks can set the entire tone of a site.

Of course, functionality is crucial. A robust navigation menu doesn't just look nice; it also adapts seamlessly to different screen sizes. I'll usually turn on Webflow's responsive previews to see how the menu collapses on tablets and smartphones. If the design calls for a hamburger icon, I'll make sure it's clearly visible and easy to tap. Occasionally, I'll style that icon to reflect the brand's palette—perhaps making it a bright accent color so users immediately notice it.

In many of my projects, I add subtle animations for that extra "wow" factor. For instance, when a user hovers over a dropdown, I might have the submenu slide down gently rather than just appear abruptly. These micro-interactions can be created in Webflow's Interactions panel without a single line of code. I prefer a shorter duration—maybe 200 to 300 milliseconds—so it feels fluid, not floaty.

Accessibility also plays a key role. A robust menu is one that everyone can use. I make sure to label my links accurately and check that keyboard navigation works correctly. If I'm implementing dropdowns, I'll verify that users can open and close them using the tab key. Webflow's default components already adhere to many accessibility best practices, which is a huge help, but I still do a thorough check.

Finally, I often convert the entire nav bar into a Symbol if the site has multiple pages. That way, any future tweak—like updating a link name or changing a background—gets applied globally with one click. This single detail has saved me countless hours of manual edits in big projects.

All told, a navigation bar is more than just a cluster of links. It's a guiding star for your site's visitors, leading them exactly where they need to go. And in Webflow, building one that's both visually striking and functionally rock-solid feels satisfying every step of the way.

CHAPTER 11: OPTIMIZING FOR DIFFERENT SCREEN SIZES

Not too long ago, I remember launching a site that looked stunning on my laptop but resembled a jumbled mess on my phone. Back then, it was a genuine struggle to make layouts adapt gracefully. But once I began using Webflow, optimizing for different screen sizes became more intuitive—close to second nature. It's an incredible relief to know that the same design can scale elegantly across desktops, tablets, and smartphones.

The first technique I embraced was starting with a fluid layout. In Webflow, I usually rely on percentage-based widths or Flex layouts rather than fixed pixels. For instance, if I'm laying out a row of product cards, I'll set them to flex-wrap, ensuring that on narrower screens, they stack neatly instead of vanishing off the edge. This approach shifts my mindset from building for a single screen size to embracing a continuum of devices.

Once I've nailed down the desktop view, I move on to the predefined breakpoints: Tablet, Mobile Landscape, and Mobile Portrait. One thing I love is how Webflow remembers my design tweaks at smaller breakpoints without affecting what I set up at larger ones. If I decide the hero text looks too big on a phone, I'll tweak the font size at the mobile breakpoint, and Webflow keeps that change unique to mobile.

Lately, I've started leveraging Grid layouts for more advanced responsive needs. With a few clicks, I can redefine how many columns display on smaller screens. Maybe I need three columns for desktop, two for tablets, and just one for phones. I used to worry about columns collapsing unpredictably, but Grid solves that elegantly. Besides, toggling between breakpoints in the Designer couldn't be easier; I just click the device icons and watch the layout adjust in real-time.

Images play a massive role in performance across different devices. A crisp, high-resolution photo might look fantastic on a 27-inch monitor, but load unnecessarily slowly on mobile. Webflow's responsive image feature helps automatically serve scaled-down images to smaller screens, which balances visual appeal with snappy load times. That's crucial for user experience, especially with visitors who may be on slower data connections.

Let's not forget about navigation. Many times, I'll create separate nav designs for desktop and mobile. A full-width horizontal menu with dropdowns may look great on a large screen but can be cramped on a phone. By setting a hamburger icon to appear on mobile, I maintain a clean, uncluttered interface. When users tap that icon, the menu slides out or appears in a way that's easy to navigate, courtesy of Webflow's interactions.

Verification is the final step. I learned the hard way that relying on one or two test devices isn't enough. Now, I'll shrink and expand my browser window, run the site through different emulator sizes, and even test it on a real tablet or phone. The goal is to confirm each breakpoint feels polished, from the largest desktop display to the smallest phone screen.

Optimizing a site for different screen sizes helps me deliver a user experience that feels thoughtfully designed for everyone. And once you get comfortable doing this in Webflow, you start seeing the web as a fluid, dynamic canvas, ready to adapt rather than break.

CHAPTER 12: INTEGRATING CUSTOM CODE SNIPPETS

I still recall the satisfaction of adding my very first custom script to a Webflow site. Even though Webflow champions a no-code approach, there are times when sprinkling a bit of custom code can open up possibilities you can't achieve purely with the Designer. Whether it's embedding a nifty animation library or adding a third-party widget, these snippets can elevate a good site into something truly unique.

Back when I was less familiar with Webflow, I worried about messing up my entire project whenever I introduced code. The good news is Webflow offers safe opportunities to integrate snippets at both the project and page levels. My rule of thumb: if the code snippet affects the entire site—like a chat widget or analytics tracking—I embed it in the Project Settings under the "Custom Code" tab. If it's only for a specific page—like a special script for a testimonial carousel—I place it in that page's settings instead.

The first time I integrated Google Analytics, it felt less daunting than I'd anticipated. I simply copied the tracking script and pasted it into the Head section of my site so that every page would include it. It was a reminder that even a line of code can amplify a site's capabilities. Analytics is just the tip of the iceberg; you can similarly embed chat services, marketing pixels, or advanced meta tags without rummaging through lines of traditional HTML.

JavaScript libraries are another game-changer. One of my favorite experiments entailed using a library for parallax effects. Although Webflow's interactions offer plenty of built-in animations, a custom library gave me a new level of creative freedom. I monkeyed around with elements that moved at different speeds as users scrolled. It felt like discovering an exciting new dimension in site interactivity that wasn't purely reliant on Webflow's default tools.

That said, I always test rigorously. Injecting custom code can introduce conflicts if not done carefully. Maybe it overrides a style or interacts with existing scripts in unexpected ways. To mitigate these hiccups, I'll publish the site to a staging domain, letting me confirm everything runs smoothly before going live. If the snippet causes layout glitches or performance dips, I can pinpoint and address them without affecting my actual domain.

Security is on my mind too. Whenever I integrate a third-party script, I choose my sources wisely, ensuring they're from reputable developers. I also keep an eye on updates. Many times, a script library might evolve, meaning I'll need to update my snippet for compatibility or performance improvements.

At the end of the day, custom code snippets are like seasoning in a recipe. Webflow gives me the main ingredients for a robust, visually compelling site, but those little bits of code can add unique flavors to keep visitors hooked. Whether that flavor is a dynamic widget or a fancy transition effect, it's empowering to know I can place just the right sprinkle of code without leaving the comfort of Webflow's environment.

Embrace the snippet, I say. It's a fantastic way to marry no-code convenience with the broader world of web development.

CHAPTER 13: E-COMMERCE ESSENTIALS IN WEBFLOW

I'll never forget the joy of launching my first online store. It was a small handmade jewelry shop for a friend, and I remember being amazed at how Webflow made it possible for two creatives—with minimal coding know-how—to build a fully functioning e-commerce site. Suddenly, tasks like product listings, checkout flows, and shipping integrations felt far less intimidating.

The process always begins with organizing the product catalog. I start by setting up Collections in the CMS, assigning fields like product name, price, and main image. This structure tells Webflow what information to pull for each listing. I especially appreciate how I can design a single product card, then let Webflow loop through the entire Collection, generating a store page filled with consistent styles. It keeps everything looking polished without forcing me to manually place hundreds of items.

Next, I design the product pages themselves. A big, eye-catching product image always goes front and center in my layouts. Below that, I like to reserve space for a descriptive paragraph, product features, and a clear call-to-action button—something like "Add to Cart" in a bold accent color. Unlike some platforms, Webflow gives me the freedom to lay out product details however I want, ensuring the aesthetic remains consistent with the brand identity.

The shopping cart is another pivotal piece. I often use Webflow's built-in cart component, which ties into the e-commerce functionality behind the scenes. With a bit of styling, that cart can match the site's overall look—no clunky out-of-place widget. The moment I tested out the shopping flow, from adding an item to finalizing a purchase, I realized how streamlined Webflow's e-commerce engine is.

One highlight is the checkout experience. Sometimes, I embed trust badges or add subtle notes about return policies to reassure the customer. Webflow's no-code approach means I can drag in text elements or icons without delving into complex code. Any special fields I need—like "gift note" or "select a size"—can be integrated right into the checkout process. By making small, thoughtful design decisions, I can reduce friction for the buyer and potentially boost conversions.

Payment gateways are vital, of course. Webflow supports popular services like Stripe and PayPal. Once configured, transactions are secure and seamless. I remember how relieved my friend was, knowing she could handle monetary transactions without wrestling with external plugins or advanced APIs. Automated emails confirming each sale also added a professional touch we both appreciated.

I can't talk about e-commerce without mentioning shipping and taxes. In Webflow, these settings live conveniently in the E-commerce dashboard. Although it's up to me to configure the rules—like flat rates or weight-based fees— the platform offers a guide each step of the way. This ensures that I don't miss crucial details, like applying the correct tax rate in a particular region.

All in all, building an online store in Webflow blends creativity and functionality in a single environment. From customizing the product pages to automating confirmation emails, each step feels integrated and polished. For anyone who's ever dreamt of selling products online without losing design flexibility, the e-commerce essentials in Webflow can be a genuine lifesaver.

CHAPTER 14: CREATING REUSABLE COMPONENTS

Back when I was putting together websites in traditional code, reusability meant copying blocks of HTML and CSS across multiple pages, hoping I didn't miss a line or break something. With Webflow, however, the concept of reusable components revolutionized my workflow. Now, I can design a helpful section—like a testimonial carousel, pricing table, or sign-up form—and quickly replicate it throughout the site without starting from scratch.

One of my favorite ways to create reusable components is by leveraging Symbols. Let's say I've built a compelling FAQ section that includes toggles and a bit of fancy styling. I package it as a Symbol, label it "FAQ Section," and drag it onto new pages wherever I want. If I spot a spelling error or want to tweak the background color, I edit the Symbol once, and all instances update automatically. This consistency is a massive time-saver.

But reusability goes beyond Symbols. I've found that a robust class naming strategy can also streamline my process. When I adhere to consistent naming—like "section-header," "section-subheader," or "btn-primary"—I can quickly apply styling across elements site-wide. It's as if the foundation is built once, then repeated with confidence. If I decide I want all buttons to shift from blue to red, I update "btn-primary," and the change cascades. It's a subtle form of reusability that prevents me from juggling countless one-off styles.

For more complex layouts, I sometimes create entire "template" pages that serve as a sandbox. Here, I'll experiment with different element groupings—perhaps a Block Quote design or a flexible Grid layout for products. Once I'm happy, I'll either turn these into Symbols or store them in a separate style guide page. This style guide becomes my personal library, always ready when inspiration or necessity calls.

I also love how reusable components tie into the CMS Collections. If I build a dynamic list for blog articles or product categories, that layout can be dropped into multiple places without me having to rebuild each layout from the ground up. Any changes to the master design are instantly reflected wherever that Collection is displayed. It encourages consistency while still letting me fine-tune each Collection item's styling.

On the collaboration front, reusability becomes even more vital. If I'm working with a team member, it's reassuring to know that the building blocks we create can be used by everyone. Less time is wasted re-creating the same design element on multiple pages. Plus, it keeps brand identity locked in, preventing random variations that might otherwise sneak in.

There's also a neat synergy between reusable components and site performance. By standardizing elements, we're often using the same classes and assets repeatedly, which minimizes loading overhead. Visitors get a cohesive, faster experience, and we as designers get a simpler maintenance routine.

Ultimately, reusability in Webflow sets the stage for efficient, scalable design. Little by little, you build a treasure trove of modular components that can be mixed, matched, and tweaked to fit any need. It's akin to having a professional toolkit at your fingertips—ready to assemble a polished project in record time, every time.

CHAPTER 15: WORKING WITH THE CMS IN WEBFLOW

I still remember the first time I ventured into Webflow's CMS, feeling both excitement and a touch of trepidation. On one hand, I'd heard that the Content Management System gave me unprecedented control over my content. On the other hand, I'd grown accustomed to the old ways of inputting text and images directly onto static pages. Once I jumped into Webflow's CMS, though, it didn't take long to realize how powerful and flexible it truly is.

Setting up my initial CMS Collections was the pivotal moment where I saw the magic come to life. Rather than manually replicating a blog post layout on every single page, I realized I could create a "Blog Posts" Collection with fields like Title, Featured Image, Author, Publish Date, and Body Content. Once the Collection was ready, I simply designed a template page using placeholders for these fields. With a handful of clicks, Webflow dynamically populated each blog post view—saving me enormous time and ensuring every post stayed consistent in design.

One aspect I found particularly liberating was the ability to tailor each Collection to my specific needs. In a project for a local art gallery, for instance, I needed to show the painter's name, artwork dimensions, medium, and even a short biography. By creating custom fields, I gave the gallery staff an easy way to update and add new artwork without ever touching the overall webpage layout. It was a huge relief for me, too, because I wasn't the perpetual gatekeeper of every little text tweak.

I also fell in love with how the CMS integrated seamlessly with static pages. Suppose I wanted to display the latest three blog posts on my homepage. Instead of manually swapping out titles and images every few days, I could just drop a Collection List onto the homepage, filter it to show only recent posts, and style it however I wanted. Whenever a new post was published, that homepage module automatically updated. In short, my site felt like it gained a life of its own—always current, always fresh.

Collaboration, too, took on a whole new dimension with the CMS. Team members could log in and access the Editor, where they could modify content directly on the live site— or at least a test environment—without touching the intricate design settings. I remember working on a fashion blog where the writer uploaded her latest articles, the stylist added relevant lookbook images, and I merely stepped in to do final checks. This streamlined workflow not only saved time but also reduced mistakes since everyone saw real-time previews of their changes.

Looking back, "Working with the CMS in Webflow" marked a milestone in my design journey. It taught me that content management doesn't have to be an afterthought or a chore. Instead, it can be a core element of the design strategy—one that empowers you and your collaborators to keep a site vibrant and up to date. Whether building a blog, a membership portal, or a product showcase, the CMS is the engine that drives consistent, dynamic content in Webflow—and it radically changed how I approach every project.

CHAPTER 16: BUILDING DYNAMIC COLLECTIONS

My appreciation for the Webflow CMS skyrocketed even further when I discovered the concept of Dynamic Collections. These Collections aren't just about storing content; they allow you to weave that content through your entire site with precision and ease. For me, it felt like unlocking a higher level of storytelling—one where even the smallest site detail could be customized and linked to living data.

I remember constructing a travel blog that required multiple categories—destinations, recommended hotels, and featured travel tips. Each category needed its own set of fields: a destination might list climate details or popular landmarks, while a hotel entry could include ratings or amenities. Webflow's Dynamic Collections let me configure these details in a structured manner. Once the Collections were set, I'd design a single template for a destination page, and suddenly I had a blueprint for dozens of locations with consistent layouts. The best part? If I ever wanted to revise the color scheme or add a new field, I'd do it in one place, and every destination page would update automatically.

What surprised me most was how flexible these Collections can be. I started by building standard text fields and image fields, but soon ventured into more specialized types, such as multi-reference fields and rich text fields. Multi-reference fields helped me link repeated data points across Collections. For instance, a single "Author" Collection could be referenced in both "Blog Posts" and "Interviews," preventing duplication of data. Meanwhile, rich text fields allowed me to style paragraphs, lists, and quotes directly— helpful for sections like long-form guides or product descriptions.

One trick I learned was leveraging Conditional Visibility. If certain fields in a Collection are empty, you can hide or display specific design elements. On a portfolio site, I used it to show a "View Live Project" button only if the link field was filled; otherwise, that button disappeared seamlessly. This minimized clutter and kept the layout feeling polished and intentional, regardless of what data was entered.

Filtering and sorting options also played a key role. Whether it was a "hot deals" section that highlighted products under a certain price or a feature grid for testimonials from specific industries, the Collection List settings let me define rules to shape how content appeared on the page. For instance, I once built a job listings page that displayed "Most Recent" openings at the top, automatically reordering them by publish date. This dynamic approach meant the site always stayed up to date, and visitors saw exactly what they needed first.

When I look back at how I used to manually piece together content with static pages, I can't help but marvel at how Dynamic Collections simplify everything. They don't just speed up your workflow; they transform how you think about each project's structure. Rather than focusing on how to place content, you're free to focus on what that content should be—and how best to guide your audience through it. With Dynamic Collections, each piece of data gains a unique purpose, and you become the orchestrator of a beautifully choreographed content ecosystem.

CHAPTER 17: DESIGNING LANDING PAGES FOR CONVERSIONS

My first foray into serious landing page design happened when I was tasked with boosting sign-ups for an online course. I felt equal parts exhilaration and responsibility. A great landing page doesn't simply look good—it compels users to act. That's when I realized that in Webflow, designing robust landing pages that convert was about harnessing both the form (visual design) and the function (user psychology).

I generally start by mapping out the user journey. Before diving into any styling, I clarify what pain point the landing page addresses, the primary benefits of the product or service, and the single action I want visitors to take—be it signing up, downloading a resource, or scheduling a call. Once I'm confident in that outline, I translate it to Webflow, relying on sections and div blocks to create distinct "chapters" of the page narrative. One section might contain a bold value proposition, the next might feature compelling social proof, and the following might reveal pricing or a deadline-based promotion.

A powerful headline remains my top priority. Something snappy—often phrased as a direct benefit—grabs the user's attention. I tend to style this text with a larger font and a contrasting color so it stands out. Right beneath, a subheadline clarifies the offering, ensuring visitors know exactly what they'll gain. If needed, I'll include a hero image that speaks emotionally to the user's needs, whether it's an image of a person achieving success or a simplified graphic metaphor.

Calls to Action (CTAs) are also crucial. I typically feature a primary CTA button "above the fold"—that first screen visitors see without scrolling. In Webflow, creating attention-grabbing buttons is as easy as styling any element. I might choose a bright accent color that contrasts with the background, and I'll add a hover effect that slightly changes color or scale, offering an interactive "nudge." Along the page, I repeat similar CTAs but in different contexts: maybe one right after a testimonial section, another near the pricing table. Consistency of style ensures users recognize these buttons as the next logical step.

Testimonials and social proof often determine a landing page's success. If I'm building it out in Webflow, I like to create a scrolling carousel of success stories or a grid of quotes and photos. By presenting authentic voices—whether they're from well-known brands or individuals—visitors sense credibility. Coupled with a countdown timer or a "limited spots" notice, it can add a sense of urgency, prompting users to act sooner.

Finally, I pay close attention to mobile design. I don't want a CTA hidden beneath screens of content on a phone. If visitors pull up the page on a small device, I want them to see relevant information and a clear call to action quickly. Using Webflow's breakpoints, I'll often trim the hero image or reduce text sizes, so the main CTA isn't buried. A carefully responsive landing page ensures potential conversions aren't lost to awkward layouts.

When everything comes together—compelling headlines, meaningful visuals, trust-inspiring testimonials, and well-placed CTAs—the page feels like an effortless journey. Visitors glide from curiosity to conviction to action in a matter of seconds. And for me, that's the best part of designing landing pages in Webflow—seeing my creativity and strategic thinking turn casual visitors into enthusiastic customers.

CHAPTER 18: INCORPORATING SEO BEST PRACTICES

The day I realized SEO could make or break a website was the day I promised myself I'd never ignore it again. I'd spent weeks crafting a gorgeous site—only to find that it languished on page three of Google search results. My content was valuable, my design was on point, but I'd overlooked the strategic aspects of SEO. When I moved into Webflow, I quickly learned that integrating best practices for search visibility isn't just doable—it's downright convenient.

I start with the basics: meta titles and descriptions. Even as I design pages in Webflow, I pop into the Page Settings to hone those crucial fields. Instead of vague titles like "Home," I craft something that captures both user intent and brand identity—like "Expert Web Design Services | Spark Innovations." It's a simple step, but it sends a strong signal to search engines about the page's core focus. The meta description then supports it, enticing users to click with a concise pitch of what they'll find once they arrive.

URL structure plays a critical role, too. By default, Webflow generates user-friendly URLs, but I always double-check. I prefer short, keyword-rich slugs—like "/web-design-tips" rather than "/838349/page1." When I create dynamic pages for blog posts, I'll map the slug to the blog title field. This way, each new post automatically gets a descriptive URL that helps both readers and search engines grasp its content.

Content structure makes or breaks on-page SEO. In my blog posts or landing pages, I break up text with headings (H2, H3) that contain relevant keywords. For instance, if I'm writing about "UI Design Trends," I might have subheadings like "Emerging Color Palettes" or "Micro-Interactions and Motion." This chunking of information not only guides readers but also gives search crawlers clear signals about each section's topic. Meanwhile, images get alt text that accurately describes the visual. Alt text not only aids accessibility—it's also another subtle clue for search engines about the context of your content.

I've learned that site speed also factors into SEO. While Webflow is generally optimized for performance, I still keep an eye on image sizes and file formats. Large hero images can bog down load times on sluggish connections. An easy fix is to leverage Webflow's automatic image compression or manually optimize in an external tool. For my more advanced sites, I sometimes integrate custom caching scripts or a Content Delivery Network (CDN), though for many projects, Webflow's default hosting handles it well.

Internal linking is another tactic that pays off. Since you can dynamically display "related articles" or "similar products" using Webflow's CMS, you build a cohesive link structure that simplifies navigation. Search algorithms appreciate these trail markers, and users are more likely to explore additional pages—improving your site's overall engagement metrics.

Finally, I track performance. Webflow easily supports Google Analytics or other SEO tools via custom code snippets. Studying which pages rank for which keywords guides my content strategy, telling me where to double down or pivot. In my experience, SEO isn't a one-time effort; it's an ongoing dance between creativity, technical optimization, and audience-building. With Webflow, each step of that dance feels far more intuitive.

CHAPTER 19: USING FORMS AND DATA CAPTURE

I'll never forget the day I finally cracked the code for using forms effectively. Before that, I'd added contact forms to sites almost as an afterthought—a simple name, email, and message field. But then came a project involving event sign-ups, where I needed more complex data capture. Rather than making me dread the process, Webflow's form builder made it feel like a creative opportunity to engage users.

The first step, of course, is dragging a Form block onto the page. Pretty quickly, I realized how easy it is to change the default fields, reorder them, or rename them in a way that resonates with the site's brand. Using the Style panel, I match the form to my color palette and typography styles, ensuring it doesn't feel like a tacked-on element but rather a seamless part of the overall design.

When I needed to collect deeper information—like T-shirt sizes, workshop preferences, or registration fees—I got a taste of how flexible Webflow's form fields can be. Checks, radio buttons, dropdowns—there's plenty of variety to suit just about any input requirement. In one instance, I set up conditional logic: if a user selected "Yes" for "Do you need hotel accommodations?" a new section appeared inviting them to select room preferences. This dynamic approach kept the form short for those who didn't need lodging, while being comprehensive for those who did.

But forms aren't just about collecting data; they're about making the user comfortable enough to part with their details. Over time, I learned to reduce friction by reducing the number of fields. When I ask for too much information, people often bail out. I also make sure to design it in an inviting way—providing clear instructions, adding a short success message, and even including a reassuring note about how I handle their data. In other projects, I integrate small details like an inline message confirming "Looks good!" for valid entries or indicating which fields are required.

Once a user hits that submit button, the data's fate is in my hands. Webflow automatically emails form submissions to my chosen address, which is great for immediate notification. If I'm working with a marketing or CRM platform, I often embed third-party integrations or add custom code to funnel the data straight into MailChimp, HubSpot, or another tool. Alternatively, for a more advanced workflow, I'll connect Zapier. That way, each submission can trigger actions—a Slack notification, a Google Sheet row, or even a Trello card for follow-up tasks. It's surprisingly simple once the pieces are in place.

My biggest revelation with forms came when I realized they could be leveraged for so much more than just "Contact Us." Want to build an email list? Offer a quick ebook download with an email capture. Need user feedback? Embed a short survey on a pop-up. In each of these scenarios, Webflow's form capabilities shine, blending aesthetic customization with robust data management. Once integrated effectively, you'll find forms are your direct line to understanding—and serving—your audience better.

CHAPTER 20: COLLABORATING WITH TEAM MEMBERS

The day I first tackled a Webflow project with a full creative team felt like stepping onto a bustling film set: everyone had a role, from content writers and art directors to junior designers eager to hone their skills. I quickly learned that Webflow isn't just a solo performer's stage—it's a collaborative environment where multiple minds can shape a site together, often in real time.

One of the biggest challenges in my early days was version control. Before Webflow, I spent way too many hours trying to manage separate design files, merging changes and ensuring no one overwrote someone else's hard work. In Webflow, though, we gained a single source of truth. I'd create an initial project, invite teammates using the Collaborators feature, and everyone could jump in with minimal risk of stepping on each other's toes. If a problem arose, Webflow's built-in backups and quick restore function acted like the ultimate safety net, letting us roll back any changes with ease.

Communication proved to be the next critical piece of the puzzle. My first inclination was to rely purely on chat tools outside of Webflow. Then I discovered the power of page-by-page notes in the Editor environment, where non-designers could flag areas that needed updates or clarify the intended copy. That immediate contextual feedback saved us all from marathon email threads. We could see the site exactly as a user would and leave comments right where changes were needed.

Task allocation also became simpler. I liked to assign roles to each collaborator so we all knew who was focused on visuals, who handled content, and who managed site settings. Here's a quick table I often share with my teams during the kickoff phase:

Team Role	Key Responsibility
Project Manager	Schedule, deadlines, and overall coordination

Designer	Visual layouts, animations, brand consistency
Content Writer	Copy, headlines, SEO-friendly text
Editor/Client	Approvals, final reviews, editorial notes

With everyone knowing their position, we were able to channel our collective strengths more effectively. And that sense of clarity let us adapt swiftly if we needed to pivot designs or rework a section.

We also used Symbols to sustain a unified look throughout the site. Once the designer and I hashed out the color scheme and typography, we saved crucial components—like headers, footers, and product cards—as Symbols. Editors had no trouble updating text inside those Symbols, which let them refine copy on the fly without accidentally changing the layout.

But collaboration isn't always about streamlined workflows; it's also about nurturing creativity. Working side by side in Webflow sparked new ideas in real time. I remember a brainstorming session in which the copywriter suggested a subtle animation on a testimonial section, and the designer was able to whip it up within minutes right in the Designer. That kind of "instant iteration" used to be wishful thinking, but in Webflow, it became routine.

By the project's conclusion, those initial jitters about coordinating multiple minds had faded into a sense of shared triumph. Each collaborator had left their fingerprints on the final product, giving our website a richness I simply couldn't achieve on my own. Ultimately, collaborating in Webflow is less about dividing tasks and more about weaving a tapestry of creativity—together, we can produce websites that are as efficient as they are inspiring.

CHAPTER 21: BUILDING MEMBERSHIP-READY SITES

I vividly recall when a client asked if their new website could include membership functionality—something beyond a simple password-protected page. They wanted different user tiers, exclusive content, and protected shopping carts for paid members. At first, I thought I'd need a complex setup or external plugins, but I quickly realized Webflow offered flexible paths to craft membership-ready sites that felt both intuitive and secure.

My starting point was the Webflow CMS. By using Collections, I could segment content based on the user level. For instance, I created "Basic Articles" for everyone and "Premium Articles" for paying members. Then, I set up dynamic pages that displayed whichever collection matched a user's membership tier. Even though Webflow doesn't have an inherent multi-login system built right in, combining it with third-party integrations gave me a robust membership structure.

That's where tools like Memberstack and Outseta came into play. With a few lines of custom code and some step-by-step setup, I learned I could layer these services atop my

Webflow design. Suddenly, I had user registration and login workflows, subscription plans, and gated content. It intrigued me how smoothly they fit into Webflow's environment, allowing me to avoid the Frankenstein-like approach so common in other ecosystems.

The design aspect was crucial too. I wanted members to feel a sense of belonging as soon as they logged in. That meant customizing "Welcome Back" messages, personal dashboards, and access links for exclusive content. Every membership tier had a slightly different look, so I used a variety of styles tied to user attributes. With a bit of creative planning, I transformed each membership tier into a brand touchpoint.

One challenge, though, was ensuring a smooth payment process for those paid tiers. Similar to how I'd set up e-commerce in Webflow, I relied on an external service's checkout flow. I embedded sign-up forms tied to my membership tool of choice. When new users selected a paid plan, the system routed them to a secure checkout, then whisked them back to my Webflow site once complete. While it required careful testing to confirm each redirect worked properly, the end result felt seamless to members— like they never left the site.

Security is paramount in any membership model. I found that robust third-party integrations handle data encryption and password hashing. Meanwhile, in Webflow, I limited public access to certain pages and Collections, ensuring only logged-in users could reach them. It felt reassuring to have the best of both worlds: a design-first approach in Webflow and a background layer dedicated to authentication and user management.

Reflecting back, building a membership-ready site in Webflow wasn't nearly as daunting as I once anticipated. By fusing the native CMS with external membership platforms, I created a gated environment that allowed me to maintain total control over the user experience. For me, it was a triumphant step forward—proof that no-code doesn't mean no options. I could still craft a personalized, secure membership journey without diving headlong into complex custom coding, and that's an exciting prospect for any web designer keen on delivering serious value to clients.

CHAPTER 22: STREAMLINING CLIENT HANDOFFS

My first professional handoff was anything but smooth. I delivered a technically sound website, only to get calls every other day from a frazzled client asking how to swap images, change text, or tweak a layout. At that point, I realized that building the site is just half the battle—ensuring the client can manage it effortlessly is the other half. Fortunately, Webflow simplified this balancing act and turned the once-nerve-wracking handoff process into something far more seamless.

I typically start by organizing each element with meaningful class names. Rather than labeling a text block "Text Block 42," I rename it "Homepage-Hero-Body." This small step is a game-changer when clients eventually poke around the Webflow Editor. It helps them see exactly what they're editing—like "Button-CTA" or "Footer-Address"—instead of scrolling through cryptic labels. Intuitive naming conventions can drastically reduce the intimidation factor.

Next, I introduce the client to the Editor mode in Webflow. Editor mode strips away the complexity of the Designer, allowing them to click directly on text or images and make updates. I schedule a brief walkthrough, showing them how to publish changes, alter blog articles, and revise pricing details without inadvertently dismantling the entire design. This interactive session usually lasts under an hour, but that investment pays dividends by cutting down on frantic phone calls and panicked emails later.

One feature that's been invaluable is the ability to restrict access. I'll set up each client with a dedicated login that only grants them Editor privileges—not full Designer privileges. This prevents them from accidentally altering layout structures or, worse, deleting entire sections. I recall once a client sincerely tried to shrink an image but ended up repositioning an entire section on the live site. Editor restrictions help avoid such mishaps, letting them focus on content updates instead.

When transferring ownership of a Webflow project, I like to ensure a complete style guide is in place. Usually, I craft a separate page that lists all the heading levels (H1, H2, H3, etc.), paragraph styles, button styles, and brand colors. The client can then visualize how each element should look and stick to consistent branding—especially helpful if they decide to add new pages or sections later.

I also encourage clients to handle site backups and version history themselves. They can quickly revert to an older variant if they regret a change. Teaching them that "Undo" is just a few clicks away can bolster their confidence in experimenting. I like to say, "Don't be scared—Webflow's got your back." This sense of freedom invites them to take real ownership of the site, which in turn can lead to a stronger long-term partnership.

Ultimately, each client handoff now feels like a collaborative baton pass—one where I equip them with the right tools, guidelines, and training for success. Rather than relinquishing responsibility and crossing my fingers, I leave them with the confidence to manage, evolve, and truly own their online presence. That empowerment not only elevates my client relationships but also showcases Webflow's remarkable potential as a platform for ongoing, client-driven growth.

CHAPTER 23: IMPLEMENTING ACCESSIBILITY FEATURES

The turning point for me came after a friend with low vision attempted to navigate one of my sites. She struggled to read the text and found certain buttons nearly impossible to identify. That single experience changed how I viewed web design forever, prompting me to take accessibility much more seriously. Thankfully, Webflow offers a variety of tools and settings that make it easier to craft experiences that everyone can enjoy.

I usually start with color contrast. When choosing my palette, I ensure there's sufficient contrast between text and background colors. Webflow's interface helps here by showing me real-time previews of how certain colors might appear. For crucial interactive elements—like links and buttons—I often use a bold hue or add a clear border. The aim is to create visuals that don't just look stylish but also remain legible for users with visual impairments.

Next, I pay attention to heading structures. For screen readers, headings are not just aesthetic choices; they guide navigation. A user might jump from H2 to H2 to get an overview of the page's content. If the hierarchy is jumbled or mislabeled, confusion ensues. That's why I map out each page's content outline early on, making sure H1 is used once at the top, followed by H2 for major sub-sections, and so forth.

Another biggie is alternative text for images. Webflow's media settings allow me to add alt text easily. This textual caption lets screen readers describe images to visually impaired users and also boosts SEO. I'll often keep alt text concise but meaningful. For instance, "Golden retriever puppy playing fetch" conveys the scene accurately, whereas "puppy1.jpg" says next to nothing.

Beyond visuals, I focus on keyboard navigation. Many users rely on keyboard-only navigation, cycling through links with tab keys. In Webflow, I check that clickable elements follow a logical tab order and that interactive widgets like sliders or accordions are functional without a mouse. Sometimes this means updating default settings or adding clear focus states—like a bold outline around the element in focus.

Forms can also pose accessibility challenges. I label every input field—like "Name" or "Email"—so that screen readers can call them out. Required fields get an asterisk alongside a textual cue explaining why they're required. For error handling, I ensure that error messages appear close to the relevant field and can be identified by assistive technologies.

Lastly, I think about continuous testing. Tools such as WAVE or WebAIM help me spot trouble spots I might've overlooked. I run these checks before final launch and keep them handy for routine audits. Every improvement I make, whether larger text or clearer forms, benefits not just users with specific needs but also the broader audience.

Ultimately, weaving accessibility into my workflow goes beyond meeting legal guidelines or best practices. It's about building inclusive experiences that treat every visitor with respect and dignity. For me, discovering how straightforward it can be in Webflow was eye-opening—I no longer see accessibility as a tedious chore, but rather as a vital, integral facet of exceptional design.

CHAPTER 24: CREATING CUSTOM ANIMATIONS WITH LOTTIE

I'll never forget the first time I stumbled upon a Lottie animation. It was this eye-catching, fluid graphic that loaded seamlessly on a webpage, making traditional GIFs and static PNGs feel clumsy by comparison. Naturally, I had to figure out how I could make something similar in my own Webflow projects. Once I discovered the Lottie integration, it felt like I'd gained a brand-new paintbrush that allowed me to add vivid movement without bogging down site performance.

The process starts outside Webflow: I typically create or source a Lottie animation using design tools like Adobe After Effects in tandem with the Bodymovin plugin. After that, I export the animation in the JSON file format. It still amazes me how compact these files are compared to video or even large GIFs. That means animations load faster, giving me more freedom to incorporate them in hero sections, interactive buttons, or even background loops without tanking page speed.

Once I have that JSON file, uploading it into Webflow is surprisingly simple. I drag a Lottie element from the panel into my design, then link to my file. Webflow instantly generates a placeholder so I can see precisely where and how the animation will appear. It took me a bit of practice to position these animations exactly the way I wanted, but using containers or absolute positioning, I found I could craft some truly striking visuals.

The real fun begins, though, when you incorporate interactions. Lottie animations can be triggered to play or pause at crucial moments—like on scroll, hover, or click. For instance, I once added a playful animated icon to a "Download Now" button. When the user hovered, the icon sprang to life, rotating and shifting colors to emphasize the action. Another time, I crafted a parallax-like effect by linking the animation's progress to the user's scroll position, so the animation progressed or reversed as they moved down the page.

I also discovered layering opportunities. Lottie elements can sit above static backgrounds or combine with other animated Webflow objects. This synergy creates a tapestry of motion that feels cohesive rather than random. Naturally,

I have to balance excitement with usability—too many animations can distract from the website's main purpose. I typically keep them short, subtle, and directly tied to user actions or narrative moments.

Optimization remains a priority. Even though Lottie files are small, I double-check that I'm only loading animations on pages that actually use them. If an animation is purely decorative, sometimes I compress it further. And just like any other resource, I test thoroughly on different devices. Some older phones or browsers may struggle with rendering complex animations, so maintaining fallback options—like a static image—helps ensure a consistent experience.

By now, using Lottie in Webflow feels second nature to me, an exciting collaboration between design and animation. Whether I'm dreaming up a lively hero section or adding micro-interactions to icons, having the power to integrate these assets so fluidly reminds me how versatile no-code tools can be. Each new Lottie animation breathes personality into a site, making visitors linger just a bit longer—and that spark of engagement, for me, is totally worth the effort.

CHAPTER 25: UTILIZING INTEGRATIONS AND THIRD-PARTY TOOLS

I can still recall the moment I realized how much more powerful my Webflow projects could become once I tapped into external integrations. Before that, I was mostly relying on Webflow's core features and sprinkling in a bit of custom code here or there. Then came a client who wanted advanced analytics, live chat, and social media feeds—all woven into a single site. This request nudged me into the realm of third-party services, and I discovered it wasn't just doable, it was delightfully straightforward.

My first step was to make sure I understood the possibilities: email marketing, chat widgets, payment processors, customer service help desks—the list went on. Rather than panicking, I found solace in Webflow's uncluttered approach to embedding tools. Many third-party providers offer snippet codes or scripts that you drop in either the project settings or on specific pages. One time I installed a chat widget by pasting a tiny code snippet into the "Before </body> tag" section, and I remember how thrilled my client was to see an instant chat bubble pop up on the published site.

One of my earliest and most beneficial integrations was email marketing. Whether it was Mailchimp or another service, linking a Webflow form to an email list was a breeze. I'd add a newsletter sign-up section, embed a bit of code, and just like that, each new subscriber's data synced into my client's marketing platform. That synergy cut down on manual exports and ensured that the list was always up to date. Over time, I learned to style form fields so they matched the site's branding, making the user experience smoother and more visually cohesive.

Analytics integrations soon became my next obsession. I'd worked with Google Analytics before, but placing the tracking code into Webflow's "Head" section felt far simpler than editing a raw HTML file. It gave me better insight into user behavior, from which pages performed best to how visitors navigated the site. If a particular landing page was underperforming, the analytics data often led me to tweak the design, move a call-to-action, or experiment with a new layout. The numbers guided creative decisions, a perfect blend of art and science.

Then, there are social media feeds, which can enliven a site by pulling in real-time content from Instagram or Twitter. Embedding these feeds brought a dose of authenticity, allowing visitors to see fresh posts without leaving the main site. It also helped brands maintain a consistent online presence, no matter which platform visitors preferred.

In my experience, one of the biggest keys to success with integrations is testing. After embedding, I always publish to a staging domain and verify that everything works: forms submit correctly, widgets load seamlessly, and the site speed remains acceptable. If any conflicts arise—maybe a widget's CSS doesn't play well with my design—I can adjust, often by adding custom styling or employing a different integration that's more compatible.

Ultimately, integrating third-party tools extends what Webflow can do out of the box. I love the feeling of crafting a cohesive digital ecosystem, combining the best of Webflow's no-code design with the power of specialized services. It's a testament to how flexible Webflow truly is— especially when you realize there's a world of possibilities that open up when you're ready to merge design, functionality, and outside innovation.

CHAPTER 26: SETTING UP A BLOGGING PLATFORM

When I first decided to launch a personal blog, I was a bit hesitant. Would I have enough content to keep readers returning? Could I make the site look fresh and engaging? But once I started tinkering inside Webflow, setting up a blogging platform turned out to be surprisingly intuitive— and way more fun than I'd ever imagined.

For me, it all began with the CMS Collections. I opened a new tab in my project settings and built one called "Blog Posts." I created fields like Title, Featured Image, Author, Publish Date, and, of course, the main Body Content. That basic structure was key to how I'd organize everything down the line. Best of all, I only had to create one design template for my blog posts; Webflow automatically applied it to every new post using that Collection.

Designing that template was a blast. I remember dragging in my heading block, specifying the "Title" field from the CMS to appear there, then placing an image element mapped to the "Featured Image" field. Below that, I used a rich text element for the Body Content. The real magic happened when I added dynamic styles—like adjusting the spacing or font size just right so that even longer posts looked polished and inviting to read.

Next, I tackled the blog listing page, the one showing all the posts at a glance. By dropping a Collection List element and connecting it to "Blog Posts," Webflow automatically populated each item with the relevant text and images. I refined it further, adding a short excerpt field so readers could get a quick preview before clicking through to the full post. It felt like building a living magazine, one I could easily reorder or sort by date or popularity if I wanted to.

One highlight for me was setting up categories or tags. I created another Collection called "Categories" with a simple name field. Then, in my "Blog Posts" Collection, I added a multi-reference field that linked to these categories. That meant I could assign a single post to multiple categories—like "Design," "Webflow Tips," or "Entrepreneurship"—and Webflow automatically handled the rest. Later, I designed category pages so that each one listed only the relevant posts. This structure keeps my blog organized and helps visitors find precisely what they're after.

Of course, what's a blog without its behind-the-scenes logistics? I used Webflow's Editor to draft posts, tagging them with categories and scheduling publish dates. Sometimes, I'd even do a couple of posts in advance, letting Webflow automatically go live on a chosen day and time. This scheduling ability helped me maintain consistency and stay ahead of deadlines.

By the time my personal blog was live, I felt a new level of confidence in mixing creativity with structured content. Setting up a blogging platform in Webflow wasn't just about listing articles—it was about crafting an immersive experience for my readers, complete with seamless navigation, striking visuals, and a sense of coherence that made the entire site feel truly professional.

CHAPTER 27: MANAGING SITE BACKUPS AND VERSIONS

Shortly after I launched my first big client project, I made a series of experimental tweaks that quickly spiraled out of control. Before I knew it, I had broken half the homepage layout. That gut-wrenching fear set in—had I just ruined weeks of work? Fortunately, Webflow's version management swooped in like a safety net, letting me restore a clean backup in mere moments.

From that day forward, I learned to see backups and version control as essential tools rather than optional extras. The process is beautifully straightforward: Webflow automatically saves a backup each time you publish your site or make significant changes in the Designer. I often head over to the "Backups" tab in Project Settings if I want to label a specific restore point. For instance, after finishing a major revamp or a big design milestone, I'll create a named backup like "Post-Redesign Layout." This gives me peace of mind: if anything ever goes sideways, I can precisely pinpoint where to rewind.

It's not just about safety, though. Sometimes version control helps me experiment more freely. I'll try out a bold new color scheme or reconfigure the navigation. If the new look doesn't pan out, I can roll back without second-guessing every step. That sense of creative freedom is invaluable—it encourages me to push boundaries, knowing I can revert in a single click if I need to.

When collaborating with teammates, backups become an unspoken hero. If multiple designers are working in the same project, it's easy for wires to cross. Maybe someone accidentally deletes a section or drastically alters a key component style. With version history, it doesn't become a blame game; we simply revert to a stable snapshot, analyze what happened, and proceed carefully. This whole system fosters a healthier team dynamic, allowing us to tackle big ideas without panicking about irreparable mistakes.

I've also taken advantage of Webflow's staging feature, particularly on complex projects. Instead of pushing changes live immediately, I'll publish to a staging subdomain, comb through the site for any quirks, and gather feedback from colleagues or clients. If everything checks out, publishing to the live site is just another click away. If not, I can revert to any stable version or make a fresh round of edits. It's the thoroughness that makes me feel like I'm operating on a professional level even when working on solo projects.

That said, a backup strategy isn't complete without good naming conventions and consistent habits. Every time I implement a big feature—like adding a new service page or embedding a new widget—I label that version. In the event I get client feedback to remove or roll back a feature, it's painless to revisit a previously labeled version.

In the end, site backups and version management in Webflow serve as both a safety cushion and a playground for creativity. They let me take design risks, collaborate responsibly, and move forward with the reassurance that no matter how wild my experiments get, I can always find my way back to solid ground.

CHAPTER 28: LAUNCHING AND HOSTING ON WEBFLOW

One of my most memorable "aha!" moments arrived when I realized just how effortless it was to launch and host a fully functional website without ever leaving Webflow. Previously, I had a laundry list of tasks: find a reliable hosting provider, configure DNS settings, manually upload files, and set up SSL certificates. Then I tried Webflow's integrated hosting for the first time and felt like someone had taken an entire day's worth of chores off my plate.

It all starts in the Project Settings under the Hosting tab. Once I'm there, I immediately see the option to add a custom domain. Whether it's a brand-new domain or one I've already purchased, connecting it is straightforward. I remember the initial time I set up a domain: I only needed to grab a few DNS records—usually an A record and a CNAME—and paste them into my domain registrar. Within an hour or two, the domain usually pointed to my site. No frantic phone calls to technical support needed.

Next, there's the matter of SSL, that little green padlock symbol that visitors love to see. Webflow provides free SSL certificates automatically. In the past, I faced complicated processes with certificate authorities and renewals, but Webflow handles it seamlessly on the backend. Knowing my projects are encrypted and secure from day one puts me at ease and impresses clients.

When it comes to performance, Webflow's hosting infrastructure is built on robust servers, complete with built-in CDN functionality. In practical terms, that means images, CSS, and JavaScript load from servers closest to the user, reducing lag times. I've had clients remark they were amazed how swiftly their site loaded once it was hosted on Webflow compared to previous platforms. Performance metrics matter for user experience and SEO, so this advantage feels substantial.

Publishing changes is a highlight too. As soon as I click "Publish," I can select whether to publish to the staging domain, the live domain, or both. I'll often push major updates to staging first, do a quick run-through, then publish to the live domain once everything checks out. Before Webflow, I remember uploading files via FTP or using other systems that felt archaic. Now, it's more like toggling a switch—simple, direct, and immediate.

I've also come to appreciate how neatly hosting integrates with the Editor. Clients I work with can pop in, make text updates or swap images, and publish those changes themselves. That sense of real-time control keeps the content fresh without bottlenecking tasks through a developer. And, in scenarios where multiple projects are in progress, I just open a different Webflow project for each site, meaning I never need to juggle multiple hosting providers or content management systems.

All told, launching and hosting on Webflow feels like the final puzzle piece locking into place. After all the design, content creation, and iterative changes, seeing the site go live without fuss is a true morale booster. It means I can shift my focus from logistics back to what really matters—refining the user experience, optimizing SEO, and celebrating the moment a new project steps onto the digital stage.

CHAPTER 29: TROUBLESHOOTING COMMON ISSUES

I'll never forget one late-night design session when I discovered my carefully configured interactions had suddenly vanished. I felt that twinge of panic, convinced I'd have to rebuild everything. But then I remembered a key principle I've picked up through my Webflow journey: challenges are inevitable, yet most hiccups have straightforward solutions if you keep a calm head and a methodical approach.

Let's start with missing or misfiring animations—that's a common snag. Often, I've found the culprit in the interactions panel, where a trigger might be incorrectly linked to an element or not set for the right class. I learned to methodically re-check each step: which element is triggered? Does the action sequence exist at the precise moment? Are any conflicting styles overriding the effect? Sometimes it's as simple as toggling "Affect: Class" to "Affect: Selected Element," instantly fixing the glitch.

Another frequent puzzle is styling that appears fine in the Designer but falls apart when published. In many instances, it's a class inheritance issue. Maybe I accidentally nested multiple classes that override each other. To debug this, I'll open the Navigator and examine the structure, or even assign a temporary background color to see which element is controlling what. Clarity often emerges once I isolate each container and div block, ensuring my margin and padding settings align with my intention.

Site performance can also raise concerns. If a page feels sluggish, my go-to diagnostic steps include checking the image file sizes—did I accidentally drop a massive 6MB photo in the hero section?—and verifying that no external scripts are bogging down load times. Webflow's built-in minification of CSS and JavaScript helps a ton, but large media files or too many embedded integrations can still hamper performance. Whenever site speed dips, it's usually solvable by resizing assets or removing any outdated scripts I forgot to clean up.

Then, there are those heartbreak moments when a layout skews on mobile. I'd pinch and zoom on my phone, spotting text that's cut off or an image that refuses to shrink. In these cases, I head to the Designer's responsive breakpoints. Often, a fixed pixel width sneaks in, or the "overflow" property is off. By switching to percentages or turning on "overflow: hidden" for certain containers, I can usually salvage the responsiveness. Another trick is checking for stray "float" properties or leftover flex settings that might be forcing content to misalign.

Sometimes, the biggest trouble is not technical but conceptual—like forgetting to define a naming convention. In that scenario, the site quickly becomes a maze of classes. For me, the remedy is to rename classes to match their function, grouping them logically, and removing anything unused. This housekeeping approach not only clears up confusion but can also enhance site performance and pave the way for easier collaboration.

Whenever I do hit a truly puzzling issue, I turn to Webflow's community forums or support guides. More often than not, somebody else has encountered a similar puzzle, and the fix turns out to be simpler than I'd have guessed. If not, posting a clear question with screenshots or a share link can lead to quick insights from other users.

Over time, troubleshooting common issues has evolved into a healthy part of my design process. Each challenge is a chance to understand Webflow more deeply—and that knowledge repeats dividends in every new project, letting me craft layouts and interactions with growing confidence and fewer surprises.

CHAPTER 30: DESIGNING FOR USER EXPERIENCE (UX)

I first realized how vital User Experience (UX) was when a colleague told me, "A stunning interface isn't worth much if users can't navigate it effortlessly." That comment shifted my focus from designing purely for aesthetics to designing with purpose. In Webflow, focusing on UX means looking beyond pretty layouts and ensuring every interaction guides visitors toward fulfilling their goals—whether that's making a purchase, signing up for a newsletter, or exploring a piece of content in more depth.

My workflow usually starts with defining user personas. Before I place a single element in Webflow, I consider who my audience is and what their expectations are. If it's a lifestyle blog, readers likely want quick access to recent articles, bold images, and maybe a multi-level category filter. On the other hand, if it's a B2B product site, the user might need a quick summary of product features, clear pricing tiers, and a frictionless path to schedule a demo. Each persona informs my design decisions—from the size of a call-to-action button to the layout of the homepage.

Next, I think carefully about site navigation. Webflow's flexibility allows me to create custom menus or interactions that align with the brand's personality, but I also remember that consistency is key. Top bars, side menus, or hamburger icons should remain predictable. If a user has to pause and think, "Where's the menu?" I've introduced unnecessary friction. Instead, I prioritize clarity—using familiar symbols and minimal sub-menu levels so visitors can easily drill down to the information they need.

I also pay attention to content hierarchy. Each page should convey what's most important in a clear, scannable manner. I often rely on headings, bullet lists, and short paragraphs to prevent information overload. For instance, on a product feature page, I'll highlight the main benefit with an H2 heading, integrate a short paragraph for context, then use a bulleted list for detailed specs. Fast comprehension is crucial; if users can't parse info quickly, they may give up.

One strategy that's helped me immensely is prototyping user flows. Before finalizing a design, I'll map out the step-by-step process a user takes—from landing page to final conversion. Maybe they start at the homepage, skim a hero carousel, click a highlighted testimonial, and eventually reach the pricing page. By walking through this journey, I can spot bottlenecks or friction points, then adjust the design to keep them engaged. The ability to wireframe or quickly rearrange elements in Webflow helps me turn these user flow maps into concrete layouts in record time.

A crucial aspect of UX is micro-interactions—those subtle feedback cues that reassure users. Think of hover states on buttons or forms that highlight valid entries in green. In Webflow, I use interactions to overlay gentle animations that guide eyes toward essential parts of the page. However, I take care to avoid overdoing it. The goal is to direct attention, not distract users with flashy effects.

Finally, there's user testing. After designing in Webflow, I share a published staging link with a small test group. Their comments often highlight issues I missed—like unclear labels, confusing form fields, or overly dense text blocks. By refining these areas, I ensure the final product delivers a smooth experience from start to finish.

Ultimately, "designing for UX" means empathizing with the visitor's journey. It's making sure every detail—from loading speed to button color—supports a user's mission. In my own projects, I've seen that when UX design is done right, viewers become delighted participants, exploring deeper and returning often. And, for me, that unwavering loyalty is what makes all the meticulous planning worth it.

CHAPTER 31: CREATING STYLE GUIDES AND PATTERN LIBRARIES

When I first ventured into building design systems, I noticed that I'd often recreate the same elements—headings, buttons, forms—across multiple pages. As soon as I realized the power of style guides and pattern libraries, my workflow changed dramatically. Instead of designing each component repeatedly, I could simply reference a centralized guide in Webflow. It was like having a master recipe book: all the ingredients for a cohesive site were right at my fingertips.

I typically start with a "Style Guide" page in Webflow, which serves as the epicenter for all global brand elements. Here, I lay out my color palette, typography scales (H1 through H6, plus body text), button styles, and fundamental components like dividers or alerts. Each item gets a clear label, ensuring that if someone else hops onto the project, they understand exactly how and when to use these elements. This eliminates guesswork and keeps the design consistent from start to finish.

For instance, if "Primary Button" is set to a bold shade of teal with white text, I keep that style locked in. Whenever I need a "Primary Button" on a new page, I simply reference that existing class. If the brand updates its primary color, I change it in the style guide, and the entire site updates automatically. That type of universal consistency not only saves time but keeps the brand identity crystal-clear for visitors.

Then there's the concept of pattern libraries. While style guides focus on details like font and color, pattern libraries are more about reusable design blocks—like hero sections, testimonial sliders, or pricing cards. In Webflow, I often craft these blocks in a dedicated page, then save them as Symbols if I plan to reuse them. This approach spares me from building the same layout repeatedly. If a client wants a consistent sign-up banner across various pages, I'll create a "Sign-Up Banner" pattern once, style it thoroughly, and then drop it into place wherever it's needed.

Over time, I've learned that a well-structured pattern library also paves the way for smoother team collaboration. If a copywriter or a junior designer needs to add a new section, they can select from the existing library instead of starting from scratch. It keeps the brand's design language consistent and helps onboard new team members more quickly.

An unexpected benefit of maintaining style guides and pattern libraries is how it aids in future-proofing. Eventually, brands evolve. They might pivot toward a new aesthetic or add fresh services. Because there's a single source of truth in the style guide, re-theming the entire site becomes far less daunting. A handful of updates can propagate across hundreds of pages, meaning that big rebrands don't send me scrambling to edit every corner of the project.

Of course, it takes discipline to keep these guides current. Whenever I create a novel component—say, a fresh layout for highlighting events—I add it to the pattern library if I suspect I'll use it again. If a brand color changes slightly, I adjust the swatch in my guide so everything remains consistent. It's a small task that pays off in spades over the lifespan of the site.

Ultimately, style guides and pattern libraries let me spend less time reinventing the wheel and more time innovating. I've found that stepping onto a solid foundation means the real creativity can flourish, unburdened by repetitive tasks or outdated elements. And in a world where brand impressions form in mere seconds, consistency can be as compelling as any groundbreaking design trend.

CHAPTER 32: INCORPORATING VIDEO AND MULTIMEDIA

The day I decided to sprinkle in a background video on a landing page was the day I realized just how powerful multimedia assets can be in elevating a site from ordinary to unforgettable. I'd always used images or illustrations in my designs, but opening the door to video and other interactive elements breathed new life into my projects. It allowed me to weave storytelling directly into the visuals, ensuring visitors felt the message before they even read a single line of text.

Video embeds in Webflow are remarkably easy. If I have a YouTube or Vimeo link, I can simply paste it into the video element, adjust its size, and let Webflow handle most of the responsive scaling. For a more immersive experience, say a background video in the hero section, I upload a short looped clip directly into the designer. Mere seconds after selecting a file, that video is playing behind the page's headline and call-to-action. When done thoughtfully, it can captivate users the moment they arrive.

Still, not all videos are created equal. One pitfall is file size. A large video can slow down a site, undermining the user experience. I've learned to optimize or trim clips, maintaining quality but pruning unnecessary frames. I also set fallback images or color overlays for mobile users who may prefer not to load a data-heavy background video. Webflow's hosting handles a lot behind the scenes, but it's worth taking every possible step to ensure performance remains snappy.

Beyond video, I've dabbled with interactive 3D models and audio snippets. An architectural firm's site I worked on featured rotating 3D building mock-ups. Visitors could click and drag to view the structure from every angle. It took a bit of custom code to integrate, but the result was a dynamic, hands-on experience that static renders couldn't match. And for a podcasting project, embedding straightforward audio players with transcripts made the site more inclusive—visitors could listen or read, whichever suited them best.

One approach I adore is layering multimedia. For instance, imagine a block where an animated GIF loops above a testimonial quote. Or a product page where scrolling triggers a series of short videos—each highlighting a different product feature. Webflow's interactions panel helps me coordinate these moments so they unfold seamlessly rather than feeling shoehorned in. Even subtle transitions—like videos fading in or auto-playing only when they enter the viewport—enhance the professional polish.

That said, I'm careful about moderation. Too many flashy elements can confuse users or overshadow the core message. I've learned to ask, "Does this video or interactive graphic genuinely add value?" If it doesn't clarify a concept or provide emotional impact, it might not be worth the potential performance hit.

No matter the medium—video background loops, 3D product demos, audio highlights—my overarching goal is to keep the narrative clear. Multimedia should work hand in hand with text and branding, not compete against them. When striking that perfect balance, a site transforms from a mere information hub to an immersive experience that remains in a visitor's memory long after they click away.

CHAPTER 33: ADVANCED INTERACTION WORKFLOWS

When I first discovered Webflow's interactions, it felt like someone had handed me the keys to a design playground of endless possibilities. I'd already experimented with hover effects and simple fade-ins, but I soon learned there was so much more beneath the surface. Advanced interaction workflows can shape entire user journeys, guiding people through a site in a way that feels intuitive, delightful, and even a bit cinematic.

One of my earliest interaction experiments was creating a multi-step progress bar that tracked how far along a user was in a tutorial. Each scroll triggered a slight animation: the bar filled by a set percentage, and the accompanying text changed to highlight the current step. This project showed me how interactions could be more than mere eye candy—they can convey key information at precisely the right moment.

I also became fascinated by "page load" and "page scroll" triggers. Setting a timed animation for elements to gracefully enter or exit can lend a professional flair to even the simplest layouts. With scroll-triggered effects, I can highlight critical info step by step, like revealing product benefits as someone moves down the page. For a product showcase site, I once engineered an effect where each scroll point pinned the hero image, enabling a descriptive text block to fade in. Visitors saw each feature in a carefully choreographed sequence, rather than all at once. It gave the site a narrative, guiding them from one selling point to the next.

Mastering these flows often requires a systematic approach. I sketch out the user journey, marking potential points of interaction. I note where I want users to pause, reflect, and pay attention to a specific message. Then I translate these moments into Webflow's interface, building timelines of animations tied to triggers. I quickly learned that naming conventions are crucial here. If each interaction step is labeled "Fade in #1," "Move up #2," it's easy to get lost. Instead, I use descriptive titles like "Hero Section Intro" or "Feature Panel Slide."

Another technique I love is combining interaction triggers. For instance, a card might scale slightly on hover, then reveal extra details on click. Or a layered background image could parallax when I scroll, while a button floats into view from the left. The synergy of multiple triggers feels dynamic, but again, cautious use is vital—overloading users with too many movements can lead to confusion or hamper performance.

I've also experimented with "infinite loops" for subtle background animations. Imagine a floating orb that slowly changes size, or a gradient background that gently shifts hue. These continuous effects can set a mood without disrupting workflow. However, I keep an eye on CPU usage, especially for older devices that might stutter if the effect is too heavy.

Ultimately, advanced interaction workflows are about shaping an emotional arc for your visitors. They progress from curiosity to engagement, and ideally, to conversion. It's part art, part structural planning. Every time I build a new effect, I remind myself that the goal is not to show off, but to deepen the connection between user and content. In that sense, interactions in Webflow are like a well-choreographed dance—everything moves in sync, supporting the broader narrative rather than stealing the show.

CHAPTER 34: DEVELOPING BRAND CONSISTENCY

I remember a short while ago, I visited a site that had a beautiful homepage adorned with a pastel color scheme and modern typography. But the deeper I navigated, the more inconsistencies I found—fonts randomly changed, buttons had alternate shapes, and banner colors shifted from pastel to neon. It felt disjointed. That experience solidified a lesson that true brand identity demands consistency, and Webflow offers the perfect toolkit to make that happen.

The first step I take in developing brand consistency is establishing core visual standards. If the brand's palette includes a cool mint green and a soft charcoal gray, I create those color swatches right in Webflow's style panel. I also define a primary and secondary font, ensuring headings, paragraphs, and quotes align with those selections. By assigning these as global styles, I avoid accidental deviations—like picking a slightly off-tone green or using the wrong font weight on a subheading.

Logo placement is another seemingly minor detail that can erode or boost brand consistency. I usually position the logo at the top-left corner of each page. Then I convert the entire navbar—logo and navigation links—into a Symbol. That way, any changes I make to the logo or brand tagline cascade across the entire site. It's a safety net against the all-too-common scenario of outdated logos lingering on certain pages.

Consistency goes beyond just color and typography. It's in the spacing, the voice of the copy, and the user flows. One of my favorite tricks is applying uniform spacing rules—like ensuring each section has the same top and bottom padding across all pages. If the hero section on one page has 100 pixels of padding, then the next page should follow suit unless there's a strategic reason to break that pattern. These subtle nuances create a subconscious harmony, making the site feel both cohesive and professional.

Of course, branding also extends to tone. The site's copy should echo the same personality—whether that's playful, formal, or adventurous. For instance, if the homepage features a casual greeting, like, "Hey there, ready to transform your business?" then I replicate that conversational approach on subpages. This continuous brand voice helps users instantly recognize they're in the same brand universe, no matter where they happen to click.

I also believe that consistency doesn't have to mean boredom. In Webflow, creative constraints can produce mesmerizing results if you know how to play within the lines. For example, a brand might rely on minimal, grayscale imagery. I can still animate those images with gentle fades and add an accent color highlight upon hover. Everything adheres to the brand guidelines while still feeling dynamic and fresh.

Finally, maintaining brand consistency includes reevaluating over time. Brands aren't static. Over months or years, a color scheme or design aesthetic might need updating. If I've established consistent classes, global color swatches, and Symbol-based layouts, implementing those changes is far less daunting. A tweak in one place ripples out site-wide, saving me from an exhaustive, page-by-page overhaul.

Ultimately, brand consistency is about trust. When visitors see the same visual language, tone, and reliability across your site, they're more likely to engage and return. And with Webflow as a canvas, it's easier than ever to ensure that any brand—big or small—stays true to its identity at every digital touchpoint.

CHAPTER 35: WORKING WITH FORMS, SURVEYS, AND FEEDBACK

I can still recall the moment I realized just how much more powerful a website could be when I started actively collecting feedback rather than simply presenting information. My sites went from one-way broadcasting channels to genuine conversation starters, all thanks to Webflow's robust form tools and a few well-placed surveys. These interactive elements don't just help me gather data; they help me refine the user experience in ways I'd never considered before.

First, there's the matter of choosing the right type of form. In simpler scenarios—like a contact form—I rely on Webflow's built-in Form block. It's straightforward to drag onto the page and style with the rest of your design. I always keep these forms minimalist: a user's name, email address, perhaps a small text box for their message. Over the years, I've learned that less friction equals more submissions. If I overwhelm them with too many fields, potential leads might bail out prematurely.

Surveys, on the other hand, call for a more methodical approach. I usually create a dedicated page or a popup overlay that invites users to share their thoughts on a new feature, report bugs, or rate the site's usability. If I'm feeling experimental, I'll embed a third-party survey tool—like Typeform or SurveyMonkey—using a small script or embed code. This way, I can leverage advanced question logic while keeping everything visually aligned with my brand. The data then syncs to my dashboard in real time, making it easy to analyze user responses and implement improvements.

Another boon of collecting feedback is that it helps me prioritize what truly matters to my users. For instance, I had a site focusing on wellness coaching. I sent out a quick, three-question survey regarding class scheduling, membership pricing, and preferred coaching topics. Within a week, the feedback revealed that prospective clients needed more flexible session times—a change I never would've guessed on my own. Adjusting my approach based on direct input not only boosted conversions but also demonstrated to my audience that I valued their opinions.

For large-scale projects, I've integrated forms with external CRMs or email marketing services. As soon as someone submits a form, their details route automatically to a software like HubSpot, ActiveCampaign, or MailChimp. That ensures my client or team receives immediate notifications and can respond promptly. I've noticed a jump in user satisfaction once I eliminated the need for them to wait days for a reply; a quick thank-you email or an auto-response acknowledging their submission can make all the difference in building trust.

Even small feedback loops can propel a site's success. I've taken to including micro-polls at the bottom of blog posts that ask, "Was this article helpful?" If enough people tap "No," I know it's time to revise the content for clarity or depth. Similarly, a star rating widget near tutorials provides an instant gauge of user satisfaction. These interactive elements subtly remind visitors that their voice shapes the site's evolution.

Ultimately, forms, surveys, and feedback mechanisms transform an otherwise static site into an evolving conversation. When users sense that their input genuinely informs design changes or product offerings, they tend to keep coming back—investing in your journey and, by extension, your brand. It's a win-win: you gather actionable insights to refine the experience, and your audience knows you're listening.

By thoughtfully placing these interactive gateways throughout my Webflow projects, I've managed to forge deeper connections with users—connections that spark loyalty, inform better services, and keep the entire design process delightfully dynamic.

CHAPTER 36: IMPLEMENTING ADVANCED SEO STRATEGIES

In my early days of designing sites, I treated SEO like a last-minute add-on: plug in some keywords here, craft a meta title there, and hope for the best. But as I honed my craft, I realized advanced SEO strategies aren't just about gaming search engines; they're about creating experiences that truly align with user intent. In Webflow, it's easier than ever to marry design excellence with the deeper layers of SEO that can catapult a site to the top of search results.

One of my go-to tactics is refining content architecture through topic clustering. Instead of scattering posts or pages around loosely related themes, I build "pillar" pages that tackle broad subjects—like "Comprehensive Guide to No-Code Web Design"—and then link out to specialized "cluster" articles that dive deeper. Within Webflow, using Collection Lists for each cluster helps me organize these topic sets consistently. By thoughtfully interlinking, search engines perceive my site as an authoritative hub on that subject, and I see more sustained organic traffic.

Another strategy involves schema markup—structured data that clarifies your site's content to search engines. While Webflow doesn't natively generate every schema type, it's relatively painless to embed the necessary JSON-LD code in your page's head section. For local businesses, I include address schemas that highlight store locations, opening hours, and phone numbers. For recipe sites, I add data about ingredients and cooking times. These rich snippets often lead to eye-catching search results—like star ratings or snippet previews—dramatically boosting click-through rates.

Page speed optimization is a must. While Webflow's hosting already scores high on performance, I try to go a step further by compressing images meticulously. If I'm embedding custom scripts, I load them asynchronously or place them in the footer so they don't stall rendering. Another trick is using Webflow's lazy loading for images, especially in blog posts with multiple visuals. When pages load blazingly fast, both users and search algorithms take notice.

I also leverage user behavior cues to refine SEO. Tools like Google Analytics or Hotjar show me where visitors are dropping off. Perhaps the bounce rate spikes on a particular page, signaling I need to rethink its content or design. For instance, I once discovered an FAQ page had a high exit rate. I restructured it into an accordion-style layout in Webflow, adding collapsible sections and embedding a short video for clarity. Soon after, bounce rates dropped, and the page started ranking for higher-intent searches in Google.

Advanced SEO also extends to how you handle international or multilingual content. If I'm designing for an international audience, I attach hreflang tags, ensuring search engines serve the right language version to the right users. In multi-language sites, I keep each language version neatly separated, either in subfolders or subdomains, making it simpler to maintain consistency across all versions.

Finally, I can't overstate the importance of content freshness. Even well-optimized articles can drift down the rankings if they're outdated. I've built editorial calendars for clients so we routinely revisit cornerstone pages, updating statistics, improving clarity, and adding new insights. This signals to search engines that the site remains relevant—a key factor in sustaining strong rankings.

All these advanced SEO strategies, integrated thoughtfully into your Webflow design process, elevate your site's visibility in a genuine, user-focused way. It's not just about snagging that top spot—it's about consistently delivering quality experiences that connect with your audience's needs, interests, and search habits.

CHAPTER 37: EXPANDING DESIGN CAPABILITIES WITH PLUGINS

Early in my Webflow journey, I recall encountering design roadblocks that made me think, "If only there were a tool for that." Over time, I discovered that the Webflow community is brimming with plugins and add-ons ready to bridge those gaps, extending the platform's native features. From integrating advanced sliders to embedding dynamic 3D objects, plugins let me push the creative envelope without a single line of code—unless I want to go there.

One of the first plugins that caught my eye was Finsweet's Attribute toolset. By adding small snippets of HTML attributes to my elements, I could create things like filterable content grids or advanced pagination. Suddenly, what I once considered a complicated coding task was as simple as copying, pasting, and adjusting a few labels. Finsweet was just my gateway. Before long, I realized there were many specialized libraries providing plug-and-play solutions for everything from dynamic accordions to multi-step forms.

Another category of plugins I've come to rely on is visual effect libraries. For example, integrating something like Locomotive Scroll can give you smooth scrolling behaviors, parallax transitions, and other interface flourishes that elevate the user experience. While Webflow offers robust interactions, these third-party scripts can help you replicate or refine design patterns typically seen on high-end agency websites. The key is to embed any required JavaScript in the project settings or page settings panel, ensuring that the library initializes with your content.

Collaboration-focused plugins also hold a special place in my workflow. Tools like Whimsical or Miro can be embedded for real-time brainstorming sessions. I once participated in a website planning workshop right on a Webflow-hosted page, using an embedded Miro board. My client and I pinned color swatches, brand guidelines, and content blocks, all in one living hub. It felt like remote collaboration had finally taken on a tactile sense of "we're in this together."

Of course, I keep a close eye on performance. Just because a plugin adds neat functionality doesn't mean I should pile on scripts blindly. Each plugin typically comes with extra load time, so I weigh the benefit against potential slowdown. If a plugin overlaps significantly with Webflow's existing capabilities, I'd rather skip it than bloat the site. In the end, thoughtful curation matters.

I also think about brand consistency. Some plugins bring their own styling, which might clash with the aesthetic I've established in Webflow. When that happens, I search for a plugin that either allows custom CSS or suits my brand from the get-go. Alternatively, I wrap the plugin's elements in a Webflow class, applying custom styling until they blend in seamlessly.

Perhaps my favorite aspect of expanding design capabilities with plugins is the sense of community innovation. Webflow enthusiasts across the globe are constantly releasing new resources—sharing them in forums, on

Twitter, or in official Facebook groups. Tapping into that energy not only propels my own projects forward but also keeps me engaged with the creativeness that defines Webflow's ecosystem.

In the end, plugins act like a secret extension of the Webflow designer's toolbox. They let me tackle ambitious ideas—interactive charts, advanced dynamic searches, or immersive media experiences—without leaving the no-code environment. Each successful integration feels like a small design victory, broadening my horizons and opening doors to new creative heights.

CHAPTER 38: PRACTICAL UI TIPS FOR MODERN WEBSITES

I remember the first time I tried to replicate a cutting-edge UI trick I'd seen on a top design blog. Back then, I wasn't sure if Webflow could handle intricate animations or sleek micro-interactions. But as I dug deeper, I found that most of those jaw-dropping interfaces rely on straightforward, time-tested best practices. Modern UI design isn't about going wild with every tool—it's about strategically deploying key elements that enhance usability and delight.

For starters, let's talk about typography. Large, bold headlines with generous line spacing instantly convey modernity. In Webflow, adjusting font sizes across breakpoints ensures that desktop users get a commanding headline, while mobile users see a comfortably smaller version. Pairing that headliner with a clean sans-serif body font keeps readability high. And if you sprinkle in subtle typographic details—like slightly letter-spaced subheadings or an elegant italic quote—the entire site feels refined yet approachable.

Next up is color usage. Many of today's sleek sites employ a minimal palette, often leaning on neutrals like off-whites or gray tones for backgrounds, contrasted with a single vibrant accent color. That accent might appear in buttons, icon highlights, or hover effects—magnifying user focus where it matters most. A color-coded system also creates an instant sense of hierarchy; whenever I see that vivid color, I know it's a clickable call-to-action or essential piece of info.

Minimalism isn't just about fewer colors; it's about intentional whitespace. My earlier designs jammed content into every corner, but once I embraced whitespace, the layouts started to breathe. Sections become visually distinct, headlines command more attention, and users naturally grasp the flow of each page. I use Webflow's margin and padding settings generously, ensuring that text and interactive elements have room to stand out without overwhelming visitors.

Then there's iconography. Flat or outlined icons persist as a hallmark of modern design. In numerous projects, I've found that consistent, icon-based cues for services, categories, or features immediately level up the polish factor. Thanks to Webflow's asset manager, it's a breeze to store a library of SVG icons and drop them in whenever needed. A cohesive icon set can tie an entire site together visually, boosting both brand recognition and usability.

In-motion design is another hallmark. However, I avoid animation overload. A quick fade-in for text blocks, a minor vertical shift on hover, or a gentle slide transition for modals can energize the experience. Tools like Webflow's interactions panel let me test different easing options—clockwise rotation, bounce, or linear—and decide which effect matches the site's tone. The trick is to remain subtle, reinforcing important content without distracting from it.

Lastly, I pay extra attention to device responsiveness. Modern UI can't neglect the mobile user. I test how each interactive element renders on smaller screens—making sure buttons remain fingertip-friendly, text is easily readable, and menus collapse elegantly. Sometimes, mobile-specific design quirks, like swipe gestures or sticky footers, can elevate an app-like feel that resonates with users on the go.

These UI tips—thoughtful typography, minimal color palette, generous whitespace, cohesive icons, subtle animations, and mobile mindfulness—work in tandem to create an interface that feels fresh yet user-friendly. And every time I iterate on these fundamentals in Webflow, I'm reminded that modern design isn't about complexity; it's about clarity, focus, and meaning.

CHAPTER 39: SCALING YOUR WEBFLOW PROJECTS

I can still picture the moment I realized my small personal portfolio built in Webflow was growing into something much bigger—a full-blown digital product library for a startup, complete with hundreds of products, blog posts, and user accounts. Scaling wasn't just a technical concern; it meant evolving the entire site while preserving its core vision and functionality. Fortunately, Webflow's framework makes it easier to go from "small and simple" to "robust and expansive" without dismantling your foundation.

One of the first scaling strategies I adopted was organizing content into the CMS from the very start. Even if I only had a dozen items, I treated them as if they'd soon become hundreds. I built Collections for products, categories, testimonials—anything that might multiply over time. This forward-thinking approach helped me avoid redoing my layouts later. Each Collection page I created was scalable by design; all I had to do was feed it more data.

Performance also comes into play as sites expand. When product catalogs swell or blog posts stack up, efficient loading becomes paramount. I rely on pagination features in Collection Lists to break content into digestible chunks. If I anticipate a massive data surge—like an e-commerce store—I sometimes set up dynamic filters or search functionality through an integration, ensuring users can quickly find what they need without endless scrolling.

Another concern is design cohesion as new sections and pages appear. Thanks to Symbols and global classes, I don't have to worry about the site turning into a patchwork of inconsistent styling. If a new category page appears, I apply the same classes for headings, buttons, and div blocks, instantly matching the rest of the site. Should the brand color palette shift, I tweak the global swatch, ensuring every instance updates in one fell swoop. It's a quick route to maintaining a unified brand identity.

Collaboration often scales up alongside content. You might bring on additional designers, writers, or even an SEO specialist. Granting each team member tailored access in Webflow helps keep the editing process flowing smoothly. Designers might work in the Designer panel, while content creators stick to the Editor, adding or updating CMS items without tampering with the site's infrastructure. This separation of duties reduces the risk of accidental overwrites and fosters a more organized workflow.

I also keep an eye on site backups and version control. The bigger a project grows, the greater the chance that a single misstep can break something important. Regularly naming key restore points, such as "Pre-launch update" or "Major product addition," offers a safety net for those moments when an experimental change needs to be undone. It's the difference between spending five minutes restoring an older version or several hours reverse-engineering an unfortunate bug.

Finally, scaling sometimes means specialized integrations. If you're adding user logins, payment gateways, or membership tiers, you might lean on third-party services like Memberstack or Zapier. They feed seamlessly into Webflow's design environment, letting your site evolve into a comprehensive online ecosystem. Pairing these integrations with well-structured collections and consistent design practices ensures that each new feature complements the overall experience.

In the end, scaling a Webflow project is about building on solid fundamentals—strong CMS organization, consistent styling, collaborative workflows, and sensible performance considerations. When done right, the leap from a small showcase to a sprawling website doesn't have to be a chaotic growth spurt—it can be a smooth journey, guided by the same design principles that made the original concept shine.

CHAPTER 40: FUTURE-PROOFING YOUR WEBFLOW EXPERTISE

I remember the day I realized how quickly the web design landscape can shift. One morning, a client asked if I could incorporate a new payment tool that hadn't even existed when I first showed them a proposal. The next week, another client wanted AI-driven chat features. It was my wake-up call that relying solely on my present skill set wouldn't cut it. Future-proofing my Webflow expertise became a top priority—and in doing so, I unlocked doors I never knew existed.

A big part of staying ahead is tracking Webflow's own evolution. I set aside time each month to watch product updates and community livestreams, jotting down new functionality in a simple spreadsheet. These features might include upgraded CMS field options, expanded e-commerce capabilities, or fresh animation tools. By applying them immediately—whether in a personal side project or a client proof-of-concept—I keep my muscle memory strong and my curiosity active.

I've also learned to treat third-party integrations like stepping stones into the future. Every time I test a novel plugin—perhaps something for advanced form logic or real-time data visualization—I gain insights into how broader web technologies pivot. Often, exploring a single integration sparks ideas for how I can combine multiple tools, resulting in unique, next-generation solutions. It's a tactic that not only impresses clients but also shields me against design stagnation.

Another factor is nurturing a vibrant professional network. Whether I'm joining live Q&A sessions or swapping tips in dedicated Webflow forums, I actively listen for patterns and challenges that other creators face. These discussions are some of the best barometers for what's on the horizon. Someone might mention a brand-new approach to membership sites or share a technique for bridging Webflow with augmented reality. When I stay visible in these circles, I'm effectively crowdsourcing my next learning goals.

Naturally, diversifying technical fluency helps too. I focus on developing an awareness—even if not deep expertise—of emerging frameworks like headless CMS or serverless functions. Investigating how they interface with Webflow fosters synergy between no-code design and more advanced stacks. Should a client someday request a multi-step e-commerce funnel that syncs with an external data warehouse, I'll already have a game plan in mind.

I've also come to value consistent personal experimentation. In my downtime, I'll try out new layout techniques or prototype unconventional animations in Webflow—features that might feel too risky for a client project. Whenever something clicks, I document the steps or transform the design into a reusable Symbol. Over time, these personal "lab sessions" fill my toolkit with distinctive elements that keep my solutions fresh and future-ready.

Finally, I've realized that future-proofing isn't just about technical chops—it's about mindset. Staying curious, welcoming feedback, and embracing a beginner's enthusiasm for every project fuels lasting growth. Each new skill or integration prompts me to reimagine what's possible in the realm of no-code. By weaving together continuous learning, community involvement, and a daring spirit of experimentation, I've forged a path where my Webflow expertise can adapt to whatever the future holds—and that sense of possibility keeps me inspired every day.